MARGARET THATCHER's poli
remarkable of modern times.
in 1925, she rose to become
western democracy. She wor
and served as prime ministe
1979 to 1990, a record unmatched ...
died on the 8th of April 2013, aged 87.

ALSO BY MARGARET THATCHER

The Downing Street Years
The Path to Power
Statecraft

On Europe

Margaret Thatcher

**WILLIAM
COLLINS**

William Collins
An imprint of HarperCollins*Publishers*
1 London Bridge Street
London SE1 9GF
WilliamCollinsBooks.com

First published in Great Britain by William Collins in 2017
This is an extract from *Statecraft* by Margaret Thatcher,
originally published in 2002

A catalogue record for this book is
available from the British Library

ISBN 978-0-00-825736-1

Printed and bound in Great Britain by
CPI Group (UK) Ltd, Croydon, CR0 4YY

MIX
Paper from
responsible sources
FSC C007454
www.fsc.org

On Europe

Contents

Contents

1

Europe – Dreams and Nightmares

THE PROBLEMS OF EUROPE

During my lifetime most of the problems the world has faced have come, in one fashion or other, from mainland Europe, and the solutions from outside it. That generalisation is clearly true of the Second World War. Nazism was, after all, a European ideology, the Third Reich an attempt at European domination. Against both, the resolve of Britain, of the Commonwealth and, decisively, of America were successfully brought to bear. A great victory for liberty was the result. The mainland Europeans benefited from an outcome which, by and large, they had not themselves secured: some have resented it ever since.

But my opening generalisation is also in a different sense true of the Cold War. Although it was above all in the Soviet Union, that is outside a narrowly defined 'Europe', that Marxism became the ideology of empire, Marxism too had European roots. Karl Marx was, it should be remembered, a European thinker in a line of European thinkers; he developed his ideas by studying the experience of Revolutionary France and, I am sorry to say, he prepared his works by courtesy of the British Museum, long before they took political shape in St Petersburg and Moscow; and it was finally the liberal democratic values of

3

the English-speaking peoples, spearheaded from Washington, which proved the ultimate antidote to communism. For a second time – for a third if you go back further to the First World War, though the issues there are somewhat more complex – salvation came from across the Atlantic.

At a personal level, I am conscious that much of my energy as Prime Minister was also taken up with Europe – and, if I had my time again, still more would have been so. Of course, Britain was not in those days fighting a war against a European power. But there was an increasingly intense struggle, all the same – one which focused on issues of great national and international significance. And, looking forward into the century which has just begun, there is every reason to imagine that this clash of aims and ideas is likely to continue.

I want, therefore, to examine now in some detail what is at stake – in this chapter from a mainly global perspective, in the next from a more narrowly focused British one. Having sketched out the problems, I shall also suggest some possible solutions. These will, however, not by and large be directed at 'Europe'. Too many British and other critics have spent too long trying to do that: it is, to speak bluntly, a waste of time, because, as I shall seek to show, Europe as a whole is fundamentally unreformable. My suggestions will thus be addressed principally to those who are still not fully party to the project, and thus not fatally compromised by it.

NEW STATES FOR OLD

For most of the Cold War period, the boundaries of Western states marked out on our atlases seemed remarkably clear, and seemed likely to last. In Asia, and still more in Africa, the situation was, of course, more fluid and confusing; though even there it was generally new names rather than new borders that

appeared, as one after the other European colonies g
independence. The greatest divide, though, was b
communist and non-communist states, with the former, wi.
ever their notional titles and dignities, falling under the sway of
the Soviet Union or China, and the latter enjoying political
sovereignty under the formal or informal protection of the
United States.

Since the end of the Cold War, however, that easily identifiable and comprehensible pattern has radically, and probably
permanently, changed. Recent years have seen more new states
emerge in Europe than at any time since the 1918–19 Versailles
and Trianon Treaties. Not that most of these were 'new' in the
sense that they lacked political antecedents. But certainly in the
former Soviet Union and in the Balkans the maps have been
redrawn in ways that still leave politicians trying to draw
breath, and cartographers in profit. This, then, has been one
feature of modern times.

Yet over the same period, another and contrary trend has
also emerged. While the countries of Eastern and Central
Europe, the Balkans and the old USSR have been trying to
establish viable national institutions, the countries of Western
Europe have been seeking to supplant and replace theirs with
international ones. The last pretences that the European Union
is an economic organisation of freely collaborating independent states are now being discarded. I very much doubt, for
example, whether any of his Continental equivalents would
echo Mr Blair's promise that he would 'have no truck with a
European superstate' and would 'fight for Britain's interests and
to keep our independence every inch of the way' – and then
advocate a European single currency.[1] Only in Britain does
anyone still peddle such nonsense and expect to be believed. A
fair-minded reading of recent history shows the way events are

...al development – the reunification of ... financial markets, war in the Balkans, ... superpower – has served as a spur to ...ted Europe. We are at or very near the ... But Downing Street seems not to have noticed.

Of course, in one sense the confusion about the European Union's true goals is understandable. No one has ever seen anything quite like it before. States, we must admit, are always to some extent artificial creations. After all, without the machinations of Bismarck there would probably have been no united Germany – at least not one based on Prussia. And much the same could be said of Cavour and his project for a united Italy based on Piedmont. Even the oldest nation states – Britain and France – are the result of deals and diplomacy and to some extent remain together because of them. States are thus the work of man, not nature.

This is even more so in the case of empires. They, above all, require able and committed elites employing skills and stratagems to sustain or expand them. Indeed, the fact that they are ultimately based on force not consent (though culture may supply some bonds in time) makes them supremely the fruit of artifice.

But how does Europe fit into this pattern? The emerging federal Europe is not, of course, a nation state.[2] It is, indeed, based upon the suppressing or, as the enthusiasts would doubtless have it, the surpassing of the concept of national identity. Its actions are often aimed at creating a kind of 'nation' of Europeans – hence the European anthem, flag, cultural and educational propaganda programmes and the like. But this process of nation-building, it is understood by all concerned, will take time. And it will certainly have to follow, it cannot hope to precede, the process of institution-building on which the Euro-enthusiasts have embarked. In fact, the EU's priority is clear: first make your government, the rest will follow.

Is the new Europe, therefore, an empire in the making? Here the parallels are closer, for its elite displays much of the arrogance and introversion of a supra-national ruling class. Yet Europe is clearly not an empire in other traditional and conventional respects. It is not a power possessed of great military might, or of over-arching technological supremacy, or of boundless resources – though again it wants to acquire or develop all these things.

Europe is, in fact, more like a state or an empire turned upside down. It lacks so much that would provide the solid foundations of statehood or imperial power that it can only exist through the satisfaction of accumulated vested interests. You only have to wade through a metric measure or two of European prose, culled from its directives, circulars, reports, communiqués or what pass as debates in its 'parliament', and you will quickly understand that Europe is, in truth, synonymous with bureaucracy. It is government by bureaucracy for bureaucracy – to which one might add 'to', 'from' and 'with' bureaucracy if one were so minded. It is not that the actual size of the EU bureaucracy in absolute terms is so staggering – at roughly thirty thousand employees it has a smaller staff than Birmingham City Council, though this figure leaves out the much larger number of national officials whose tasks flow from European regulation. No: what makes Europe the ultimate bureaucracy is that *it is ultimately sustained by nothing else*.

The structures, plans and programmes of the European Union are to be understood as simply existing for their own sake. Europe thus provides a new variation on Descartes' 'I think therefore I am': in its version 'I am therefore I do' – though, like other multinational bureaucracies, it gets round to doing rather less and less effectively than it intended. Pope John XXIII was once asked by a visitor to the Vatican how many people worked there. He answered: 'About half.' This reflection may be applied to Europe too.

The movement towards a bureaucratic European superstate – for no other term adequately serves to describe what is emerging – has huge implications for the world as a whole. Yet I am repeatedly struck on my travels outside Europe by just how little understanding there is of this. At least until recently, the main attention which the issue received in America or in the Far East related to the nuts and bolts of trade agreements. And when successive British governments – not least that which I led in the 1980s – were seen to be at odds with the rest of Europe, and particularly with the dominant Franco–German axis, that was put down merely to the quirks of history or to the ordinary jostling of national interests.

That perception is now changing, particularly in Washington. And not a moment too soon. It is one of the great weaknesses of reasonable men and women that they imagine that projects which fly in the face of commonsense are not serious or being seriously undertaken. The creation of the new European superstate is a case in point. It is time for the world to wake up to it; if it is still possible, to stop it; if it is not, to contain and cope with it.

THE EUROPEAN IDEA

Bismarck, who makes several appearances in these pages and whose opinions on such matters should be taken seriously, knew exactly what to make of appeals to European idealism. 'I have always,' he observed, 'found the word "Europe" in the mouths of those politicians who wanted from other powers something they did not dare to demand in their own name.'[3] This too has been my experience.

The concept of Europe has always, I suspect, lent itself to a large measure of humbug. Not just national interests, but (especially now) a great array of group and class interests happily disguise themselves beneath the mantle of synthetic European idealism. Thus we find an almost religious reverence for 'Europe' accompanied by a high degree of distinctly materialistic chicanery and corruption. I shall try to explain the low-mindedness later. But here it is the high-mindedness that accompanies it which concerns me, because it is actually the more disturbing in its consequences.

It is often said that the origins of the European project should be traced back to the post-war determination of a number of Continental European politicians, officials and thinkers to build a supra-national structure within which future wars in Europe would be impossible. To this end, France and Germany would be locked together, initially economically, but by incremental steps politically too. And, of course, this impulse was indeed historically important. It was the basis of the first stage of the European plan – the European Coal and Steel Community established on 18 April 1951 – conceived by Jean Monnet and Robert Schuman. It was then manifested in the famous (or notorious) preamble to the Treaty of Rome, signed on 25 March 1957, which sought 'ever closer union'. And it has persisted and grown in strength up to the present day, when a federal European superstate is on the verge of creation. One should add that this was not the *only* impulse at work throughout that period: it was not, for example, my goal, or as I then believed the Conservative Party's goal, in the seventies, eighties and nineties. But the fact is that it is the ideas of

Monnet, Schuman, de Gasperi, Spaak and Adenauer – not those of Thatcher (or even de Gaulle and Erhard) which have ultimately prevailed.[4]

My point here, however, is that the impulse to create a European superstate was not simply that of avoiding war in Europe. It was a good deal older than that. Nationalism is often condemned as providing an excuse for the persecution of national minorities. But *supra*-nationalism should be still more suspect, because it provides a doctrine for the subjugation of whole nations. So it has proved in Europe. At the height of its power in the sixteenth century, the Habsburg Holy Roman Empire, for example, aspired to universal domination. The initials A-E-I-O-U (*Austria est imperare orbi universo* – Austria is destined to rule the whole world), the Habsburg motto, famously summed up that ambition. But, in practice, it was only partially and fleetingly realised. Then for a still briefer period, though with much bloodier thoroughness, Napoleon Bonaparte bestrode the continent of Europe. It is not simply that the language was French which makes the Napoleonic programme for European unity seem so contemporary. For example, among Bonaparte's aims was, he said, to create 'a monetary identity throughout Europe'. He later claimed that his common legal code, and university and monetary systems, 'would have achieved a single family in Europe. No one would ever have left home while travelling.'[5] The President of today's European Central Bank could hardly have put it better.

Adolf Hitler can with good reason be seen as following in Napoleon's footsteps in his ambitions for European domination. Indeed, the Nazis spoke in terms that may strike us as eerily reminiscent of today's Euro-federalists. Thus Hitler could refer contemptuously in 1943 to 'the clutter of small nations' which must be eliminated in favour of a united Europe.[6]

It is not, of course, my suggestion that today's proponents of European unity are totalitarians, though they are not well-known for their tolerance either. What we should grasp, however, from the lessons of European history is that, first, there is nothing necessarily benevolent about programmes of European integration; second, the desire to achieve grand utopian plans often poses a grave threat to freedom; and third, European unity has been tried before, and the outcome was far from happy.

In reply to this, it will certainly be said that the purpose of today's projected European political union is quite different, because it is not to be achieved by force, and because its proclaimed rationale is to preserve peace. But this argument is no longer convincing, if indeed it ever was.

It is surely questionable whether either the European Coal and Steel Community, or the European Common Market, or the European Economic Community, or the European Union – let alone the incipient European superstate – played or will play any significant role in preventing military conflict. A defeated, divided and humiliated Germany was not in any position to cause trouble during the Cold War years – and it is a very long time indeed (since Napoleon, in fact) since any power *other* than Germany ever caused wars in Europe. The threat during the Cold War was, rather, from the Soviet Union, and it was an American-led NATO, not European institutions, which preserved Western Europe's peace and freedom. Even today, it is still true that an American military presence in Europe is the most important guarantee of the Continent's security, both in the face of threats emanating from the former Soviet Union and from any renewed German ambitions – not that I wish to exaggerate those dangers at present either. Finally, it does seem to be stretching the pacifist credentials of the Euro-enthusiasts beyond credibility to maintain that a united Europe is necessary to keep the peace, when it is energetically seeking to become a major military power.

The idea of Europe would, though, not have as powerful resonance if it was merely associated with cartels, Commissioners and the Common Agricultural Policy. As someone who has come to be profoundly disillusioned with and suspicious of all that is done in the name of 'Europe', I fully recognise this. The European myth is no less powerful for being that – a myth. And its power stems from its association in many people's minds with most of what goes to make up civilised living. For example, the contrast is often made, particularly in France, with the alleged vulgarity of American values. In the eyes of many Euro-enthusiasts, Europe vaguely represents ideas of law and justice that stem from the Greek and Roman eras. For the aesthetically minded, it is Gothic cathedrals, Renaissance paintings and nineteenth-century classical music that hold sway. The European idea is, it seems, almost infinitely variable. Therein lies its appeal. If you are pious, it is synonymous with Christendom. If you are liberal, it embodies the Enlightenment. If you are right-wing, it represents a bulwark against barbarism from the Dark Continents. If you are left-wing, it epitomises internationalism, human rights and Third World aid. But the fact that this portentous concept of Europe is so infinitely malleable means that, in truth, it is simply empty.

'Europe' in anything other than a geographical sense is a wholly artificial construct. It makes no sense at all to lump together Beethoven and Debussy, Voltaire and Burke, Vermeer and Picasso, Notre Dame and St Paul's, boiled beef and *bouilla-baisse*, and portray them as elements of a 'European' musical, philosophical, artistic, architectural or gastronomic reality. If Europe charms us, as it has so often charmed me, it is precisely because of its contrasts and contradictions, not its coherence and continuity. It is difficult to imagine anything less likely to be moulded into a successful political unit than this extraordinarily uneven mix of unlike with like. I suspect that in actual fact even the most fanatical Euro-enthusiasts have, in their heart of hearts, understood this. They keep quiet about the fact and would protest the opposite, but actually they do not like the day-to-day human reality of Europe one bit. That is why they want to harmonise, regulate and twist it into something altogether different, rootless and shapeless that can be made to fit their utopian plans.

THE EUROPEAN ECONOMIC AND SOCIAL MODEL

To the extent that there is a 'European' identity it can best be perceived in what is often described as the European economic and social model. This model, though it comes in several somewhat different shapes and sizes, depending upon the politics of the Europeans concerned, is clearly distinct from and indeed sharply at odds with the American model. In order to illustrate the philosophy behind it, and so as not to confuse it with old-fashioned socialism, one can profitably consider some words of Edouard Balladur, the then French Prime Minister: 'What is the market? It is the law of the jungle, the law of nature. And what is civilisation? It is the struggle against nature.'[7]

M. Balladur is an extremely sophisticated and intelligent right-of-centre French politician. But he clearly understands nothing about markets. Markets do not exist in a void. They require mutual acceptance of rules and mutual confidence. Beyond a certain level, only the state, setting weights, measures, rules and laws against fraud, profiteering, cartels and so on, can make markets work at all. Of course, the market – any market – implies limits upon the power of the state. In markets the initiative comes from individuals, the prices reflect supply and demand, and the outcomes are, by necessity, unpredictable. But to describe the operation of markets as barbaric shows a particularly shallow and unrealistic understanding of what constitutes Western civilisation and underpins Western progress.

In France, the hostility to markets – and particularly to the international markets through which nations trade with another – is very deep-rooted. It may be that there is something in the French psyche which reacts better than the British to a large measure of state control and high levels of regulation. Certainly, the quite successful performance of the French economy in recent decades might confirm that.

But the European economic model also has a German variant, and this, given Germany's size and wealth, is the more important one. Whereas the French prefer statism – they invented the word, after all – the Germans incline to corporatism. They are not anti-capitalist, but their conception of capitalism – sometimes referred to as Rhenish capitalism – is one in which competition is limited, cartels are smiled upon, and a high degree of regulation is provided. Another aspect of this system is revealed by the term 'social market'. This expression was coined by Ludwig Erhard,[8] though I believe that he later came to dislike it because it was used to justify too much state interference and expenditure. For Germans nowadays it implies the provision of more generous social benefits than anyone in Britain, apart from those on the left of the Labour Party, would normally consider appropriate to a 'safety net'. And indeed the Germans are still wrestling with the need to curb that spending.

What both the French and the Germans can agree upon, however, is that the sort of economic policies pursued in

America, and to a large extent in Britain since 1979, are unacceptable. Thus, writing in *Le Monde*, the French and German Finance Ministers proclaimed: 'The obsessive insistence of the neo-liberals on the deregulation of labour markets has contributed more to the blocking of reforms than to the creation of jobs. We are convinced that the European social model is a trump card, not a handicap.'[9]

In fact, a number of authoritative studies have quite convincingly proved the opposite. Examining the impact of moves in France and Germany to stimulate employment by limiting working hours, Keith Marsden noted that at the same time as the average number of hours worked had fallen, the two countries' unemployment rates had risen. By contrast, in the United States where people were working longer, and in Britain where working hours had remained stable, there had been significant falls in unemployment. Similarly, early-retirement programmes in Europe had not made available more opportunities for younger workers: rather, the effect had been to increase social security taxes to support the retired – so burdening business. Finally, Mr Marsden noted:

> There is a clear correlation between higher government expenditure and lower employment. In the US, the government share of GDP was twenty-two percentage points below that of France but its employment ratio was fifteen points higher. Britain's public spending level was eight points below Germany's, yet its employment ratio was seven points higher.[10]

Another study of Europe's social model by Bill Jamieson and Patrick Minford has highlighted the main economically harmful features of the European model: higher state spending, higher overall taxes, higher social security contributions – noting particularly the damaging burden this places on business – higher corporate taxes and higher levels of regulation, especially of labour markets. The results have been eminently predictable, but as an example of wilful self-damage no less shocking all the same: 'The contrast with the United States is stark. Since 1970 the US economy has created almost fifty million new jobs, while the EU has created just five million.'[11]

GOVERNMENT SPENDING AND UNEMPLOYMENT

Government spending as a percentage of GDP/levels of unemployment as a percentage of the labour force, 1999

	GDP	*Unemployment*
Britain	39.1	6.1
Germany	45.9	8.8
France	52.1	11.3
Italy	48.3	11.3
Euro Area	46.8	10.0
USA	30.0	4.2
Japan	38.1	4.7

Source: *OECD Economic Outlook*, December 2000: Annex Table 28

EUROPE'S PENSIONS CRISIS

Another way of describing the difference between the European and the American models is to borrow a rather profound observation of Friedrich von Hayek. In *The Road to Serfdom*, first published in 1944, Hayek wrote:

[T]he policies which are now followed everywhere [in Europe], which hand out the privilege of security, now to this group and now to that, are nevertheless rapidly creating conditions in which the striving for security tends to become stronger than the love of freedom. *The reason for this is that with every grant of complete security to one group the insecurity of the rest necessarily increases.*[12] [Emphasis added]

The European model epitomises precisely this: it places security above everything else, and in its persistence in eliminating risk it inevitably discourages enterprise. That is the basis of Europe's pensions crisis, whose full implications are still not widely grasped.

Of course, in one sense the cause of the crisis is demography, the failure of much of Western society to reproduce. One can speculate about the causes for this and what it may tell us of contemporary values, attitudes and institutions. One can also debate whether and how policies might be changed to reverse long-term demographic decline. But such discussions, fascinating as they are, are irrelevant to the crisis much of Europe is facing *now*.

No less a person than the EU Commissioner in charge of the Internal Market and Taxation, Frits Bolkestein, has admitted that Europe faces a 'pensions time-bomb'. He has noted that the ratio of workers to pensioners will decline from four to one to less than two to one by 2040. And he observes that if unfunded pension liabilities were shown up in the national accounts of some member states this would represent a debt of over 200 per cent of GDP.[13] Italy is the EU country which is facing the worst crisis. It has a fertility rate of just 1.2, the lowest in the world, and also the world's most costly pensions system, amounting to over 15 per cent of GDP – 33 per cent of worker payrolls, expected to rise to 50 per cent by 2030.[14]

Continental European countries have walked into a trap from which there appears no painless exit. Of course, they could not know just where demography would lead. But they have known well enough for some years that the promises implicitly made to pensioners could not be afforded. It was precisely because we realised the implications for Britain's public finances that in 1980 we ended the connection between the retirement pension and incomes (it now rises in line with prices). And in 1986 we cut back state funding of the State Earnings-Related Pension Scheme (SERPS) and provided incentives to opt for private-sector Personal Pension Plans (PPPs). As a result, future state obligations have been curtailed to manageable levels. Britain also now has more money invested in pension funds than the rest of Europe put together. Although other EU countries have made repeated attempts to scale back their social liabilities, none has taken similar substantial steps. As a result, just three countries – the United States, Britain and Japan – possess three-quarters of the entire world's funded pension assets.[15]

Quite how the countries of mainland Europe are going to cope with their problems is unclear. But someone is going to be disappointed – either pensioners or workers. And it seems that the official figures actually understate the scale of that disappointment. This is because it is not enough to express the problem in terms of national finances: it can only be understood in terms of equity between the generations. There is nothing theoretical about this. If one generation is expected to carry an excessive burden on behalf of another it will seek by every means to avoid it. It will either demand that past promises are broken, or it will not work, or it will not pay its taxes, or the most talented people will leave. Socialist governments which have tried to tax 'till the pips squeak' have ample experience of that. It is the main reason why even left-wing governments today try to keep marginal tax rates down. In the present case, and employing the concept of 'generational accounts' – which 'represent the sum of all future net taxes (taxes paid minus transfer payments received) that citizens born in any given year will pay over their lifetimes, given current policy' – Niall Ferguson and Laurence J. Kotlikoff have made various projections of the changes required to achieve 'generational balance'. The scale of what is implied is illustrated by the conclusion that, for example, nine EU countries would need to cut government spending by more than 20 per cent if they wanted to rely on this means to achieve balance.[16]

THE COMMON AGRICULTURAL POLICY AND PROTECTION

Europe's pensions problem is relatively recent. By contrast, its agriculture problem is of long standing. Although the European Common Market had its origins in a project to create a common policy towards coal and steel, it was the Common Agricultural Policy (CAP) which from the time of the Treaty of Rome was the central pillar of the structure.[17] Political leaders and their policies come and go. Reform programmes rise and fall. But the CAP goes on for ever. No one seriously seeks to justify it. The days when we were told that without it Europe might be short of food have long since passed. Despite successive attempts at reform, not least those initiated by Britain, the CAP is wasteful, environmentally damaging and extremely costly. It still absorbs some £30 billion – about half of the EU's total budget.[18] But it continues because it constitutes the most important reason why the less industrially developed European countries put up with other European programmes that diminish their competitiveness, and it is the unspoken reason why so many new countries want to become members.

The CAP puts up the cost of food for EU consumers, thus increasing our costs and reducing our growth. It also depresses food prices worldwide, as subsidised European food exports deprive farmers in poorer countries of their livelihoods. This is precisely the wrong way round. Industrialised countries need low-cost workforces; agricultural countries need to provide their peasants with incomes. Both lose from the CAP.

The CAP is also a force for global protectionism. It has been estimated that the CAP is responsible for 85 per cent of the world's agricultural subsidies.[19] Not surprisingly, this prompts widespread resentment. Other countries, aware of this scandalous situation, are thus less willing to make compromises and resolve disputes.

The EU is not the only body which subsidises agriculture and it is not the only trade grouping which is inclined to protectionism. But on both counts it is certainly the most serious global offender. It has been estimated that the total annual cost of the CAP to the world economy is about $75 billion, of which two-thirds is borne by the Europeans in the form of higher prices, inefficient production and economic distortions. The rest falls on non-EU countries through lost agricultural export opportunities.[20]

Another expert study has found that the EU economy is almost as protected as it was a decade ago. Thus Professor Patrick Messerlin calculates that the cost of this protection, across the board, is equivalent to about 7 per cent of the European Union countries' GDP, some $600 billion.[21]

The European tendency towards protection – demonstrated not just in the operation of the CAP but in numerous trade questions: films, bananas, and hormone-treated beef – is inherent in the European project itself. The reluctance to engage in open trade with the outside world only reflects a reluctance to accept the working of open markets at home. The EU and its predecessors were never, it should be remembered, interested primarily in free trade as such. They were and are a customs union – that is a group of countries which, while allowing free trade among themselves, charges a common set of tariffs to the rest of the world. The level of these tariffs has fallen sharply from an average of 12 per cent to 3 per cent over the last forty years as part of international trade negotiations. But the concept of global free trade is one to which the European countries have never been wedded, and never will be.

In theory, fundamental reforms of the CAP might, if they ever came about, remove one of the main reasons why the EU is such a force for protectionism. But the combination of high taxes, high levels of regulation and so high costs on the one hand, and the inflexibility resulting from a single currency and interest rate on the other, will in any case press Europe further down the protectionist path. Even within the framework set by the World Trade Organisation, there are many ways in which the EU could provide covert protection for its producers – such as through 'anti-dumping' measures. The EU's trading partners must expect that it will do everything that it can to exploit such loopholes.

As the European superstate emerges on to the world scene, it will be keen to flex its muscles in economic as in other matters. It will seek to combat the 'neo-liberalism', i.e. the belief in free markets, which the French and German Finance Ministers so roundly denounced in *Le Monde*. It will try to substitute a more highly managed, i.e. more bureaucratic, model on international trade and finance. The Europeans will ultimately fail. But 'ultimately' can be a long time. Meanwhile, they spell trouble.

WIDER STILL AND WIDER …

In such circumstances it might seem odd that the EU is besieged by countries seeking membership. The shortcomings of the system are, after all, there for all to see. Yet enlargement is still the topic most talked about in European circles – at least in public.

Thus the alleged rationale of the Nice Summit in December 2000 was to prepare for further enlargement of European Union membership. It was argued that increasing the number of member countries from fifteen to twenty-seven required institutional reforms which would allow more streamlined decision-making, i.e. loss of the national veto.[22] One can see how that fits the federalist agenda. What is increasingly contestable, however, is the sincerity with which EU countries view enlargement.

During the 1980s and most of the 1990s, Britain was in the forefront of those urging a widening of Community membership. As Prime Minister, I was keen to see the former dictatorships of Spain and Portugal given the opportunities and the stability required for democracy to flourish. Both I, and later John Major, were even keener to widen membership to include the former communist countries of Central and Eastern Europe, for very much the same reason. The extension of the frontiers of a free and prosperous Europe to the east was an integral part of the programme of a Europe of cooperating nation states which I had put forward in my speech at Bruges in 1988 – where I reminded my audience that 'we shall [for which read 'should'] always look on Warsaw, Prague and Budapest as great European cities'. After the fall of the Berlin

Wall the following year this argument became even more cogent. To prolong the division of Europe by an economic tariff wall once the old political wall dividing West and East had crumbled was manifestly unjust.

Yet this is precisely what the European Community did. Far from welcoming in the former communist countries – with the exception of East Germany, which joined the West with hardly a by-your-leave – they were left to the tender mercies of agricultural dumping under Europe's CAP and a niggling system of trade quotas. Twelve years after the collapse of communism, Poland, Hungary, the Czech Republic and the rest are still waiting.

Enlargement of the Community eastwards has traditionally been attractive to both the British and the Germans, but has been a good deal less so to the French and to the countries of Southern Europe. There is no great secret as to why this is so. Alongside our wish to see the ex-communist countries encouraged to create successful Western-style economies, British governments have hoped that, as the EU jargon has it, 'widening' would be at the expense of 'deepening'. With the prospect of enlargement to include as many as twenty-seven members – counting in all the candidate countries – it seemed to us a plain impossibility to proceed with creating a federal super-state. The differences and potential conflicts between the members would be just too great.

For the Germans, extension eastwards had a rather different attraction and reflected other geopolitical interests. As a revealing CDU/CSU paper, 'Reflections on Europe', of 1 September 1994, put it:

The only solution which will prevent a return to the
unstable pre-war system, with Germany once again
caught in the middle between East and West [a
somewhat eccentric description of the Third Reich in
the thirties!], is to integrate Germany's Central and
Eastern European neighbours into the European post-
war system and to establish a wide-ranging partnership
with Russia ... If European integration were not to
progress, Germany might be called upon, or be tempted
by its own security constraints, *to try to effect the
stabilisation of Eastern Europe on its own and in the
traditional way.* [Emphasis added]

By contrast, the French have, with the limited exception of
Romania, not sought out friends or clients in Eastern Europe.
Moreover, France and even more so Greece, Spain and Portugal
have been extremely wary of the impact upon the CAP, and the
valuable benefits they receive from it, of the introduction of
new members with large, primitive agricultural sectors.

For as long as the Germans continued to be enthusiastic
about the entry of the ex-communist countries, some (albeit
snail-paced) progress was made. But it is now apparent that
resistance within Germany to expansion is growing. The
German EU Commissioner for Enlargement, Günter
Verheugen, has, for example, suggested that a referendum may
be needed in Germany before enlargement goes ahead. German
public opinion appears to be quite strongly opposed to the
prospect of free entry for goods and services and, above all,
workers from the East. In particular, hostility to early full
membership for Poland has hardened.[23]

The present British government is, it seems, still strongly in
favour of early expansion. But one may question whether this

policy still makes much sense. All that has been seen of developments within the European Union over the last decade confirms that 'deepening' – that is the persistent accumulation of more and more powers by European institutions to override national wishes and interests – will go ahead, however much membership 'widens'. Indeed, as was shown by the decisions made at Nice, even the vague prospect of enlargement provides the excuse for a raft of new measures of centralisation. Similarly, the long-standing British hope that the need to absorb new members would lead to fundamental reform of the European Union's finances, above all the CAP, shows every sign of proving illusory.

For all these reasons, I am now unpersuaded by the case for further EU expansion. And although I fully understand the mix of historical, political and economic factors which account for the enthusiasm of the Central and East European countries for full membership, I also doubt whether they are well-advised to press for it on the terms available. Since leaving office, I have had the benefit of many frank and friendly (and that in the proper not diplomatic sense) conversations with senior political figures from these countries. Most of them, when pushed, are uneasy about what the EU may entail. Having endured the best part of half a century living under socialist bureaucracy, and seeing their national identities and rights overridden, they are not at all keen to be ruled from Brussels. Furthermore, although many of them are deeply uneasy about instability to the east, and so still want the reassurance offered by EU (as well as NATO) membership, they have few illusions about the degree to which Europe is dominated by Germany. And that too worries them, though they are not likely to admit it publicly.

European politicians and officials are wont to talk rather patronisingly of how far the applicant countries have yet to go in modernising and opening up their economies in order to prepare for entry. But what really alarms the Europeans is their *own* lack of preparedness in the face of low-cost competition. If as part of their preparations for entry the former communist countries are willing to tie themselves up with all the rules and regulations imposed by Europe, they will finish up by giving away much of the competitive advantage they currently enjoy. At which point, presumably, their slower growth rates could be used in order to justify putting off membership once again. In my view, the applicant member countries would therefore be well-advised to consider long and hard whether full membership of the European Union is what they really want. Negotiating free-trade agreements with the EU and with the North American Free Trade Area (NAFTA) – and, indeed, with Britain (on which, see the next chapter) – might suit their interests better.

So I believe that:

- The old arguments for expansion of EU membership no longer apply
- The EU should be pressed to concede free-trade arrangements with the applicant countries
- It should also be pressed to stop undermining these countries' agricultural sectors by dumping its products at their farmers' expense
- The governments of the applicant countries would be wise to find other ways to modernise their economies and expand their markets – ones which do not involve loss of sovereignty, the acceptance of German dominance, or piling costs on their industries.

DEFYING DEMOCRACY

The EU-applicant countries ought also to be aware of the prevailing style of politics within the European Union. This style is difficult to sum up in one word: it is, in fact, an unusual mix of the authoritarian, the bureaucratic and the interventionist on the one hand, with the compromising, the uninspiring and the ineffective on the other. The European Union is for ever awash with plans, programmes and projects. But the result, more often than not, is an inefficient muddle. Its leaders' eloquence is hyperbolic. But their decisions are characterised by horse-trading. Its ambitions to assert itself as a great power are unmatched. But the means at its disposal are few, and its attempts to play a role on the world stage have been universally embarrassing.

Perhaps the most significant shortcoming of the fledgling superstate is that it is not, will not be, indeed ultimately cannot be, democratic. This has nothing to do with the much discussed 'democratic deficit', which usually refers to the alleged disparity between the power wielded by the Commission and that wielded by the European Parliament. In fact, this is based on a false premise. The Commission and the Parliament share the same federalist agenda – and it is not democratic.

The *real* reason why there can be no functioning pan-European democracy is because there exists no pan-European public opinion. No matter how many attempts are made to create links between the political parties of different European countries, those parties know that they have to campaign upon, and that their fortunes will be determined by, national programmes and issues. The impact of European questions on such elections is most likely to be negative – when something that the European Union favours, such as open borders or more immigration, prompts popular anger.

It is a commonplace, but it is all too frequently ignored, that the European Union nations are extraordinarily deeply divided by language – no fewer than twelve main languages are widely spoken among the present members.[24] Even those educated elites which speak foreign languages with reasonable facility may well be a long way from sharing the thought patterns of native speakers of those languages. And it is still the case that for the great majority of Europe's population, 'home' is to be described in national, or local, not Continental terms.[25]

Of course, in time Europeans may all, in any case, speak English (I only half jest).[26] If that happens, it might be possible to consider seriously trying to make democracy work at a pan-European level. But for the present, and indeed for the foreseeable future, the more decisions which are made at a supra-national rather than a national level, the more remote and thus the less democratic Europe will be.

Moreover, none of the various schemes being put forward to give Europe a new 'constitution' can alter this. It is no surprise to me that the strongest proponents of Euro-federalism today often first cut their political teeth in the infantile utopianism, tinged with revolutionary violence, of the late 1960s and the 1970s. Some people are instinctively wrong about everything – even when they reverse their position. Thus the German Foreign Minister, Joschka Fischer, revelations of whose activities when a young left-wing radical have alternately entertained and shocked the German public, on 12 May 2000 in Berlin gave his views about what he called 'the finality of European integration'. Herr Fischer's answer to current problems was:

> the transition from a union of states to full
> parliamentarisation as a European Federation ... And
> that means nothing less than a European Parliament

and a European government which really do exercise legislative and executive power within the Federation. This Federation will have to be based on a constituent treaty.

He continued by arguing for:

[C]ompleting political integration … [through] the formation of a centre of gravity. Such a group of states would conclude a new European framework treaty, the nucleus of a constitution of the Federation. On the basis of this treaty, the Federation would develop its own institutions, *establish a government which within the EU should speak with one voice on behalf of the members of the group on as many issues as possible, a strong parliament and a directly elected president.*[27] [Emphasis added]

And just in case anyone thought that this was merely a little provocative kite-flying, the whole package was later endorsed by others. President Jacques Chirac in a speech to the German Bundestag argued for the establishment of a 'pioneer group' of European countries led by France and Germany, committed to deeper political integration.[28] Chancellor Schröder went on to call for the European Commission to be transformed into 'a strong European executive' with an elected head – in effect a European government.[29] Then Lionel Jospin, the socialist French Prime Minister, provided his own gloss on the federalising project. Although his ideas differed in some respects from those of the German Chancellor – he wanted more economic regulation and less power for the Commission – M. Jospin was all in favour of a 'European government of the euro-zone'.[30] The

Franco–German (though now it might be better to call it Germano–French) axis thus clearly remains in good order, despite all hopes and fears to the contrary. And it is an axis which Britain is unable effectively to resist – even if the present British government wished to do so.

The planned erection of this vast federal superstructure would amount to nothing less than the building of a new European superstate. It is empty sophistry to deny this and instead to call it a 'superpower', as Tony Blair insists upon doing.[31] I shall give a copy of my memoirs to anyone who can provide a credible description of a European superpower which is not a superstate. Somehow I think I shall still have a few volumes in stock.

As I have already explained, unless and until there comes to exist a genuine European-wide public opinion, which in turn would involve the evolution of a genuine European-wide sense of identity, there are deep-seated reasons why Europe cannot be democratic. But if this argument should strike some as a little theoretical, one can turn instead to the ample evidence provided by European politicians' and officials' demonstration of their contempt for ordinary democratic procedures. The following examples should suffice.

The Germans know that perhaps the greatest symbol of their post-war achievements was the Deutschmark, managed with such exemplary skill and integrity by the German Bundesbank. So, not surprisingly, most of the population wanted to keep those arrangements. In 1992 opinion polls showed 84 per cent of the German public in favour of a referendum on the Maastricht Treaty. And almost 75 per cent opposed the loss of their currency.[32] But there was no referendum, and the Deutschmark was duly abolished in favour of the untried euro. The German political and business elite closed ranks and the wishes of the majority went for naught. They still do: opinion polls taken in March 2001 showed 70 per cent of Germans opposing the introduction of the euro.[33] But nobody seems to care.

Similarly, when the Danes – who were actually permitted a referendum – voted to reject Maastricht on 2 June 1992, the response from Europe and Denmark's pro-European political elite was that they should keep on voting until they came up with the right answer. For good measure, Britain's Foreign Secretary of the day, Douglas Hurd, warned that voting 'no' once again would result in Denmark's 'isolation' and could provoke a 'crisis affecting Denmark's position within the EC'.[34] The Danes, thus browbeaten, dutifully reversed their earlier decision and on 18 May 1993 meekly voted 'yes'.

But Brussels, like all bullies who initially get away with it, kept on threatening the Danes and eventually went too far. The outrageous threat of Pedro Solbes, the European Commissioner in charge of Economic and Monetary Union, in March 2000 to the effect that 'Part-time membership of the EU is not good enough: in the longer term it's not possible to be in the Union and outside EMU [Economic and Monetary Union],' cut no ice with Danish voters in their referendum that September.[35] Fifty-three per cent of them defied the warnings and rejected the single currency. But we may be sure that the Eurocracy will be back.[36]

They certainly will in Switzerland. The Swiss have flourished mightily outside the European Union. They have enjoyed prosperity, stability and liberty, and one might be forgiven for thinking that no one would be foolish enough to want to upset that happy state of affairs. But the Europeans and the pro-European Swiss federal government do not see it that way. In a referendum on 4 March 2001 77 per cent of the Swiss voted against membership of the EU. Indeed, not a single canton voted in favour. Nevertheless, the federal government continues to reaffirm its intention of seeking EU membership in the next five to ten years.

Countries like Switzerland and the states of Central and Eastern Europe would be well-advised to study the EU's treatment of Austria – as the Danes did when pondering their vote before the latest referendum. In October 1999 Austrians voted to end the old, corrupt system of power- and perk-sharing between left and right. Fifty-four per cent of voters supported the Austrian People's Party and the Austrian Freedom Party. There was no suggestion that the election was rigged. It was perfectly peaceful. The right-wing Freedom Party, under its then leader Jörg Haider, won its 27 per cent of the vote fairly and cleanly. However, the left-dominated EU Council of Ministers, with opportunistic support from President Chirac, imposed political sanctions on Austria in the hope that the Austrians would be prepared to put the left back in power. Various insensitive utterances by Herr Haider were adduced to confirm that Europe was faced with a threat from right-wing extremists. But it seems likely that the Freedom Party's scepticism about the merits of European integration was at least as important in earning the EU's disapproval. Doubtless, the Europeans thought that little Austria would quickly buckle. But the imposition of sanctions turned out to have quite the opposite effect. Austrians who had no love for Haider rallied round the government. There was deep anger. The EU saw that it had overreached itself and worried about the effects on the forthcoming Danish referendum – rightly as it turned out. A face-saving formula was adopted and after a report by three 'wise men' the sanctions were quietly dropped on 12 September 2000.[37]

The bungled attempt to override the wishes of the Austrian people in order to achieve a national government of a political complexion pleasing to the EU member states was a highly significant indication of the shape of the future. Moreover, Chancellor Schröder's cack-handed threat levelled at Italy, at the height of the Austrian crisis, to the effect that similar action would be taken to stop the right winning power there did not go unnoticed – particularly in Italy.[38]

The truth is that Silvio Berlusconi and his Forza Italia party, with the Northern League and the National Alliance parties, represent everything that the left-wing power-brokers of the EU fear and loathe. Signor Berlusconi is a dynamic businessman, not a recycled bureaucrat. He and his partners are strongly anti-communist. His programme is based upon liberating enterprise from state control. The House of Freedom coalition is a moderate conservative grouping, whose approach is similar to that of conservatives in Britain and the United States. Yet it is too much for the left-of-centre Euro-federalists, who deeply distrust Signor Berlusconi's commitment to their grand project of burying nation states in a superstate. A concerted Europe-wide media campaign of vilification, the like of which I have rarely seen in politics, was launched against Signor Berlusconi to intimidate the Italian electorate into backing the left. I was infuriated by this, and lent my support to him and his colleagues in an open letter I wrote to the Italian press. It concluded: 'This is not the first such Europe-wide attempt to bully national electorates. But it may turn out to be the last – if Italy refused to bend the knee.'

The piece was widely reported and perhaps it did some good. At any rate, Italians voted heavily for the House of Freedom parties, and the Berlusconi government, as long as it keeps together, now has a real chance of turning Italy into an efficient, prosperous, modern state.

In the case of Italy – a major European country, one of the original Six – the EU's predominantly left-wing governments were prudent enough to refrain from direct threats of sanctions. But we should not assume that this would be the attitude if a smaller country – another Austria – dared to vote in parties that the EU thought undesirable. Indeed, the EU has now given itself still more power to undermine or override political parties and democratic choices it does not like. It was at Amsterdam that the Council of EU Ministers was given the authority to decide on 'the existence of a serious and persistent breach' of the principles of 'liberty, democracy, respect for human rights' etc. by a member state, and then to suspend some or all of that member state's rights (Article 7).[39] At Nice, Europe's power to threaten those whose policies its majority of governments did not like was significantly extended, by qualifying the language used at Amsterdam so that now the Council of Ministers might decide that there was 'a clear *risk* of a serious breach' (emphasis added). Thus, by degrees, the accretion of central powers and the draining of national democratic choice proceed.

The counterpart of the EU's lack of democracy is a lack of accountability. There is simply not sufficient public interest in the conduct of European politicians and high officials to place it under continuing effective scrutiny. The resulting remoteness is a recipe for abuse of power, misuse of public funds, and in some cases straightforward corruption.

One has only to read the damning conclusions of the 'Committee of Independent Experts' on allegations of fraud, mismanagement and nepotism of 15 March 1999. They speak of:

a loss of control by the political authorities over the
Administration that they are supposed to run
(paragraph 9.2.2)

instances where Commissioners or the Commission
as a whole bear responsibility for instances of fraud,
irregularities or mismanagement in their services or
areas of responsibility (paragraph 9.2.3)

a 'state within a state' ... allowed to develop
(paragraph 9.2.8)

use [of] Community funds (sometimes illegally) to
ensure a match between the objectives to be achieved
and the resources to be employed (paragraph 9.4.3)

[its] becoming difficult to find anyone who has even
the slightest sense of responsibility (paragraph 9.4.25).

None of this is at all surprising. If you combine within a single
system centralised decision-making, a culture of secrecy, and
the elimination of genuine debate about ends and means you
can hardly complain at the ensuing graft and incompetence.
This is not going to change even if you seek out and appoint
people of the highest morals and deepest standards of probity.
And it will not be cured either by technical and procedural
reforms of the sort since put forward by European Commission
Vice-President Neil Kinnock.

Indeed, as is the way in Europe, the problems created by
extensions of unaccountable central power always seem to
justify further such extensions in order to deal with them. Thus
the response to the scandalous levels of fraud in the EU has
been to propose the creation of a European system of criminal
law and procedure to deal with fraud against the Community
budget, in effect the kernel of a federal criminal justice system.
This system, known to the initiated as 'Corpus Juris', would

create a European Public Prosecutor with a delegate in each capital city. A set of special national courts working under common European rules would issue 'European arrest warrants' and could incarcerate potential defendants for extended periods without trial at the request of the Prosecutor.[40]

Jury trials would be excluded from these special courts, and the proposed Europe-wide definitions of the offences of fraud are both unclear in scope and considerably wider than would be recognised under British law. There is little doubt that this is intended to be the thin end of a very thick wedge. It should be understood in the light of the provisions in the Treaty of Amsterdam which commit EU members to an 'approximation, where necessary, of rules on criminal matters' and to 'common action on judicial cooperation'.[41] All these proposals are still at an early stage. But with the decision at the Tampere summit in October 1999 to set up EUROJUST – a body of prosecutors, magistrates and police officers detached from each member state – and with the current proposals to create a 'European judicial space', there is little doubt that they will in one form or another materialise.[42] Considered alongside calls for the expansion of Europol into a Europe-wide version of the FBI, this is very much the shape of things to come – when the Euro-federalists eventually get their way.[43]

I conclude that:

- There is no way in which the EU can be made 'democratic': the pursuit of this illusory aim is in fact likely further to reduce the power of national electorates
- Equally, there exists no programme of reforms which can make the EU's politicians and officials genuinely accountable

- The best that can be done at present by Britain and those other member states which value their own democracy is to oppose the bullying and abuse of procedure which the EU favours – no matter against whom those tactics are levelled.

EUROPEAN CURRENCY – PROGRAMME FOR A SUPERSTATE

The most substantial manifestation of the design to create a fully-fledged superstate so far is the European single currency.[44] This project is essentially political, rather than economic. The power to issue a currency is a fundamental attribute of sovereignty, not some symbolic or technical matter. Indeed, it is not for nothing that in past centuries infringement of that right by counterfeiters was reckoned as something akin to treason and punished accordingly. The truth is not concealed by the modern Continental proponents of the euro, who on this as on other related matters have been a great deal franker than their British counterparts.

> We want the political unification of Europe. Without monetary union there cannot be political union, and vice versa (Ex-Chancellor Helmut Kohl)[45]

> The introduction of the common European currency was in no way just an economic decision. Monetary union is demanding that we Europeans press ahead resolutely with political integration (Chancellor Gerhard Schröder)[46]

The introduction of the single currency is not primarily an economic but rather a sovereign and thus eminently political act (German Foreign Minister Joschka Fischer)[47]

The Council of Finance Ministers of the eleven euro-zone nations will become the 'economic government of Europe' (Former French Finance Minister Dominique Strauss-Kahn)[48]

The single currency is the greatest abandonment of sovereignty since the foundation of the European Community by the Treaty of Rome … When it is asserted that the step must also lead to political union, something logical is being said and something fundamental is being forgotten. The conclusion is logical because it is impossible to leave it at that and take no further steps. It is forgotten, though, that this decision is of an essentially political nature, because it is the abandonment of one of the distinguishing marks of sovereignty which define our nation states (Former Spanish Prime Minister Felipe Gonzalez)[49]

We now need an economic government of the euro-zone (French Prime Minister Lionel Jospin)[50]

All these people ought to know. They should be heeded. Without the power to issue and so to control one's own currency – and by 'control' I include the generally desirable aim of letting it float freely – a state can no longer be said to determine its own economic policy. It can no longer set its interest rates in line with monetary conditions and other requirements: instead, interest rates are set for it by a supra-national authority according to supra-national criteria. A state's ability to cope with economic shocks or to respond to economic cycles is thus very much constrained. It is, consequently, forced to rely on fiscal means alone to ride out difficulties.

But precisely because there has been a fundamental shift of power and authority to the supra-national (in this case European) level, individual countries using the single currency are not going to be allowed to spend, tax and borrow as they and their electors like. It is an illusion to think that fiscal and monetary authority can ever in the long run be politically separated – after all, even 'independent' national banks which set interest rates are ultimately responsible to the political institutions from which they derive their authority. The Maastricht Treaty's assurance that 'a member state shall not be liable for or assume the commitment of central governments, regional, local or other public authorities, other bodies governed by public law or public undertakings of another member state' is not where matters will or can end.[51] There will not just be a single currency in euro-land: there will be a single balance sheet. Already we see this in the form of the so-called Stability Pact, effectively imposed by Germany as a condition for allowing European economic basket-cases into the euro. The Pact places limits beyond the Maastricht criteria on what countries can borrow and imposes heavy fines for those which break the rules. Combined with the drive for tax harmonisation stemming from a distorted interpretation of the Single Market, such pressures on individual countries to hand major fiscal decisions to the European authorities will eventually turn member states into more or less the equivalent of local authorities. Thus the vision of Maastricht's 'Europe of the Regions' will be fulfilled.

I believe that:

- The European single currency is bound to fail, economically, politically and indeed socially, though the timing, occasion and full consequences are all necessarily still unclear
- It therefore follows that countries which have not already joined the project would be well-advised to keep out
- This failure cannot be rectified by American or other international attempts to rescue the euro, because the fundamentals of euro-land are irremediably unsound
- The most important priority for the non-Europeans is to see that European policies do as little harm as possible now or later to the world economy.

EUROPEAN ARMY – PROGRAMME FOR A 'SUPERPOWER'

As I have noted, the European superstate is also designed by its architects to become a superpower. The roots of this aspiration lie deep in French soil. France has for many years wanted to see an alternative military power to an American-led NATO. The European Union's plans for a separate integrated European defence have provided the French with a unique opportunity to achieve this goal. These plans only saw the light of day, however, because Tony Blair's government has reversed the traditional British – and indeed its own earlier – opposition to them. It did so at Saint-Malo in December 1998, not for any identifiable security consideration but rather in order to burnish its Euro-credentials at a time when the retreating prospect of sterling's entering EMU was calling them into question.

At Saint-Malo the British and French governments broke new ground by agreeing that the EU 'must have the capacity for autonomous action, backed by credible military forces, the means to decide to use them, and a readiness to do so, in order to respond to international crises'. To this end the EU would 'also need to have recourse to suitable military means ... *outside the NATO framework*'[52] (emphasis added).

In furtherance of these plans, an EU summit at Helsinki in December 1999 established the goal of being able to deploy within sixty days, and to sustain for at least a year, a force of up to corps level (sixty thousand soldiers), with the necessary command, control and intelligence capabilities, combat support services and additionally, as appropriate, air and naval elements. To provide the recruits for this European 'Rapid Reaction Force' (ERRF), a pool of some two hundred thousand troops would probably be required. Needless to say, this was a huge undertaking.

By the time of the Nice summit in December 2000, the project had taken still clearer shape. The Presidency Report on European Security and Defence Policy, whose conclusions were endorsed at Nice, contains some deliberate ambiguities required for British domestic consumption and inserted at British request in order to reassure the Pentagon. Thus on the one hand, the Report notes of the plan: 'This does not involve the creation of a European army.' Yet on the other hand at every stage it makes clear that something very like a European army is indeed involved. It says that the aim 'is to give the European Union the means of playing its role fully on the international stage'. It emphasises that among the Rapid Reaction Force's tasks will be to act as 'combat forces in crisis management, including peacemaking'. It states that there will be established on a permanent basis a European Political and Security

Committee, a Military Committee, and a Military Staff. Among the operating principles mentioned are 'preservation of the Union's autonomy in decision making'.

What does all this verbiage really mean? It seems to me to suggest very strongly that far from serving to strengthen the European contribution to NATO, the EU countries under French inspiration have deliberately embarked upon the creation of at best an alternative and at worst a rival military structure and armed forces.

Of course, there are limits to what the Europeans are likely to achieve acting alone. But these limits are ones of practicality, not of policy. Thus it would in practice be impossible for European forces to be deployed effectively in a 'peacemaking', i.e. combat, role – as in the Balkans for example – without depending upon US intelligence, heavy-lift capabilities and high-tech weaponry. In this sense, the European Rapid Reaction Force may well have a short and undistinguished career – neither European (it will be dependent on US support), nor Rapid Reaction (it will not be able to deploy quickly), nor indeed much of a Force. And the old problems of all multinational intervention forces – different languages, decision by committee, divided authority, competing objectives – will be gravely worsened by the absence of what still makes NATO effective, namely American leadership.

Tony Blair, on his first visit to Washington to see the new President, gave Mr Bush (as the latter confirmed) various assurances about the new force, among which were that 'the planning [of ERRF operations] would take place within NATO' and even that there would be 'a joint command'.[53] Similarly, Geoff Hoon, the British Defence Secretary, has promised that 'the EU will not divert resources from NATO, duplicate its arrangements, create separate military structures, or conduct operational planning'.[54]

I do not understand how these assurances can be squared with what the text of the agreement endorsed at Nice actually says. Nor do I see how it is compatible with the objectives of the French and other backers of the project. General Jean-Pierre Kelche, France's Chief of Defence Staff, has stated that 'there is no [NATO] right of first refusal. If the EU works properly, it will start working on crises at a very early stage, well before the situation escalates. NATO has nothing to do with this. At a certain stage the Europeans would decide to conduct a military operation. Either the Americans would come or not.'[55] Hubert Védrine, the French Foreign Minister, has called for the EU force to have its own 'elements of operational planning' and 'its own capability', while General Gustav Hagglund, the Finnish Chairman of the EU's permanent Military Committee, has declared the ERRF to be an 'independent body' and not 'a subsidiary of NATO'.[56]

The French and those who think like them have been so insistent on achieving an autonomous European defence capability precisely because they see it as constituting a vital attribute of a new European superpower which will rival the United States. So how Mr Blair imagines that he can honour the assurances which he gave to President Bush I do not know. But if he fails to do so he will turn out, through one foolish and frivolous initiative, to have done more harm to the trans-Atlantic relationship than anything since the Suez Crisis of 1956.

As for President Bush, I believe that he was wise at this first meeting to take what Mr Blair said at face value. He carefully phrased his 'support for [Mr Blair's] point of view' on the basis of the specific assurances which he had received. But if I had been the British Prime Minister, I would have taken equal note of Mr Bush's answer at the same Washington press conference to a question about China, whose intentions the Americans have, of course, every reason to doubt: 'I think you've always got to begin with trust until proven otherwise.' The operative word is 'until'.

We shall soon see who is right. If the Europeans truly wish to improve their NATO contribution they can show it simply enough. They can increase defence expenditure. They can move swiftly to establish professional armed forces, like those of the UK. And they can acquire more advanced technology. Indeed, unless that happens soon the gulf between the European and US capabilities will yawn so wide that it will not be possible to share the same battlefield.

Alas, I do not think that sharing battlefields with our American friends – but rather disputing global primacy with them – is what European defence plans are truly about. And Britain should never have been party to them.

It is already clear that:

- The fundamental impulse towards a separate European defence is political rather than military
- That impulse, stemming as it does from the French, is also one of rivalry not collaboration with an American-led NATO
- The chances of Britain's transforming the initiative into something different are now slim – though we should still try
- Any European army (by whatever name) will be of limited effectiveness and heavily dependent on the US
- But the project could still damage the cohesion of the Alliance, as senior figures in the US administration have warned

- Unless we can be sure of preventing that, Britain must pull out of Europe's misguided military schemes.

A STATE IS BORN?

In their different ways, Europe's plans for a single currency to rival the dollar, its furtive but rapid moves to create its own armed forces to substitute for those of NATO, its ambition to create a common judicial area which will intrude upon national legal systems, and the current project of devising a European Constitution at the centre of which will be an elected European government all betoken one of the most ambitious political projects of modern times. Its authors are fully aware of this. The obvious parallel is with the creation of the United States of America. Hence the use by Euro-enthusiasts of the expression 'United States of Europe'.[57]

The parallel is both deeply flawed and deeply significant. It is flawed because the United States was based from its inception on a common language, culture and values – Europe has none of these things. It is also flawed because the United States was forged in the eighteenth century and transformed into a truly federal system in the nineteenth century through *events*, above all through the necessities and outcomes of war. By contrast, 'Europe' is the result of *plans*. It is, in fact, a classic utopian project, a monument to the vanity of intellectuals, a programme whose inevitable destiny is failure: only the scale of the final damage done is in doubt.

But it is also, for these very reasons, significant to Europeans and non-Europeans alike. It seems very likely that the drive for a United States of Europe, a European superstate, is now unstoppable. Of course, something may still occur to derail it. The Americans might call the European bluff on plans to provide an alternative to NATO. The single currency might be buffeted by external shocks and internal dissent, and so collapse. There is even a slight possibility that in either France or Germany – the countries that matter in this respect – the rush to abandon national democratic institutions in favour of bureaucratic European ones might be halted by electoral pressures. Nothing is inevitable – even in euro-land. But I very much doubt whether any of these things will in fact occur. The momentum is just too strong.

It remains for the non-European world, above all America, to try to reduce the harm the new Europe is set to do – and then when the folly falls, as through lack of common interests it finally will, to help pick up the bits. The choice that remains for Britain, though, is rather different – as I shall now explain.

2

Britain and Europe – Time to Renegotiate

BRITAIN'S EUROPEAN EXPERIENCE

It is frequently said, indeed it has become quite a mantra, that Britain missed the European 'train' and thus was unable to exercise the requisite influence upon its eventual destination.[1] The lesson drawn from this, naturally enough, is that Britain must from now on take part in every new European venture in order to avoid that happening again, and so as to exert maximum 'influence'. Yet the more we learn about and have the opportunity to reflect upon the history of the European project, the less convincing even the first part of that thesis appears.

The story of the modern drive for European integration, although as I have noted above it had significant precedents, has really to begin in the 1950s.[2] The attitude of the British government towards the European project in the post-war years was, truth to tell, somewhat ambiguous. In particular, the words of Winston Churchill can be subjected to different interpretations.

On many occasions Churchill waxed lyrical about the prospects of European unity. But it was less clear what exactly he envisaged would be Britain's role. At The Hague in May 1946 Churchill thus expressed the hope 'that the Western democracies of Europe may draw together in ever closer amity and ever closer association'. He saw 'no reason why, under the guardianship of the world organisation [i.e. the UN], there should not ultimately arise the United States of Europe, both those of the East and those of the West, which will unify this Continent in a manner never known since the fall of the Roman Empire'. Yet in the same speech he noted that 'the affairs of Great Britain and the British Commonwealth and Empire are becoming ever more closely interwoven with those of the United States, and that an underlying unity of thought and conviction increasingly pervades the English-speaking world'. How were these grand and opposing concepts in practice to be reconciled?[3]

A year later, speaking in the Albert Hall in London, Churchill again addressed the same theme and indeed talked of the 'spiritual conception of Europe'. He went so far as to say that 'if Europe united is to be a living force, Britain will have to play her full part as a member of the European family'. And, in what must surely be considered a rhetorical flourish from this independent-minded patriot, he even warned that 'without a United Europe there is no sure prospect of world government'. Yet when it came to practicalities, the security architecture which he favoured in his speech turned out to be quite different:

> In the Constitution [of the UN] agreed at San
> Francisco, direct provision was made for regional
> organisations to be formed. United Europe will form
> one major regional entity. There is the United States
> with all its dependencies; there is the Soviet Union;
> there is the British Empire and Commonwealth; and
> there is Europe, with which Great Britain is profoundly
> blended. Here are the four main pillars of the world
> Temple of Peace.[4]

In truth, even in his most visionary moods, Churchill does not seem to have envisaged Britain's ever being part of the United States of Europe, however much he thought that she should encourage and contribute to it. As early as 1930, writing in the New York *Saturday Evening Post* with regard to then current federalist ideas, he expressed his underlying conviction:

> The attitude of Great Britain towards unification or 'federal links' would, in the first instance, be determined by her dominant conception of a United British Empire. Every step that tends to make Europe more prosperous and more peaceful is conducive to British interests ... We have our own dream and our own task. We are with Europe but not of it. We are linked, but not comprised. We are interested and associated, but not absorbed.[5]

In the post-war years this remained his view. Nor should it be dismissed as short-sighted or unrealistic. Churchill was quite right at this time to see Britain as enjoying a unique international position that also gave her unique strengths. She lay within three interlocking circles – those of the Commonwealth, the Anglo–American relationship, and Europe. And that was an excellent strategic vantage point, exploitation of which required a large measure of freedom of action. Any yielding up of British sovereignty to a federalising Europe was thus necessarily ruled out. So it is doubly understandable that once Churchill returned as Prime Minister in 1951 he toned down his European rhetoric and continued the approach of the previous Labour government, keeping Britain out of both the European Coal and Steel Community and the European Defence Community. Accordingly, in terms very similar to those of his article of 1930, we find Churchill speaking in the House of Commons in 1953 posing a rhetorical question:

> Where do we stand? We are not members of the European Defence Community, nor do we intend to be merged in a Federal European system. We feel we have a special relation to both. This can be expressed by prepositions, by the preposition 'with' but not 'of' – we are with them, but not of them.[6]

Nor, incidentally, did Churchill's views towards Europe mellow into nostalgia towards the end of his life. Andrew Roberts, one of the best historians of the period, notes how 'by 1962 Field Marshal Montgomery found [Churchill] sitting up in bed smoking a cigar, shouting for more brandy, and protesting against Britain's proposed entry into the Common Market'.[7]

But by then the world had changed in three important respects. The first, and most significant, was the jolt that had been given to British self-confidence by the Suez fiasco of 1956. One can argue the pros and cons of the Suez operation, and I well remember taking part in those debates at the time.[8] But the conclusion drawn by most of the British political classes was understandable – that Britain could no longer rely on the United States and that, as the Commonwealth adopted a diminishing political importance, it was necessary instead to join the European Common Market or, more precisely, the European Economic Community (EEC). The second contributory factor was the recognition that the EEC 'Six' (France, West Germany, Italy, Belgium, Holland and Luxembourg) were making greater economic progress than anyone had previously predicted. In retrospect, this hardly seems surprising: national economies devastated by war, in which the workforce is well-educated and highly motivated, are almost bound to enjoy very healthy rates of growth as they recover. But at the time, Britain, bogged down by restrictive practices that had increased in wartime, envied the European record. Europe seemed to offer a way out of our difficulties, one all the more attractive because it avoided facing up to the need to make painful reforms. The third factor, following on from this, was that the European Free Trade Area (EFTA), in which we had placed high hopes, was quite soon widely – and fairly or unfairly – seen to be something of a disappointment.

Harold Macmillan, Prime Minister after Anthony Eden's resignation in the wake of Suez, was in any case an enthusiast for Europe. Yet he was a subtle and pragmatic one. His appreciation of geopolitical realities even now deserves respect, whatever one thinks of his conclusion. This is illustrated, for example, by his statement to Cabinet in April 1961 after his return from discussions in Washington. The minutes (thus in indirect speech) record the Prime Minister's sentiments:

> In recent years, the communist bloc had been gaining ground at the expense of the West and, if this was to be checked, the leading countries of the Western world would need to draw more closely together. There was, however, a risk that current developments in Europe would tend in the opposite direction; for, if the countries of the Common Market formed a close political association under French leadership, this would create a further political division in Europe and would also have a disruptive effect within the Atlantic community. This might be averted if the United Kingdom, together with some of the Seven [i.e. EFTA], could join the political association of the Six and help to

build in Europe a stable political structure which would prevent France now, and Germany later, from attaining too dominant a position.[9]

Macmillan encapsulated in these words what might be called the Atlanticist argument for Europe. It was one which had just been pressed on him particularly hard by the United States. And it would become the basis of that steady pressure which Britain has faced – at least until very recently – from America to integrate itself ever further into Europe.

In some respects the argument was persuasive. It was true, after all, that the West needed to hold together in the face of Soviet encroachments. A prosperous and cooperative (Western) Europe could from this point of view help to win the Cold War against the East. In Washington it seemed then and later that Britain, by throwing her weight behind that cooperation (and incidentally by benefiting from the resultant prosperity), could be a crucial counterweight to France, then under the wayward and prickly leadership of General de Gaulle. The echoes of that period reverberated until very recently around the American State Department. I strongly suspect that they still do in the British Foreign Office and in Downing Street – long after Anglo-Saxon hopes and Gallic fears that Britain could reshape Europe became largely redundant.

At this time, therefore, Paris almost as much as Moscow was seen by Washington as 'the problem'. But, paradoxically perhaps, it was de Gaulle and not Kennedy, or even Macmillan, who best grasped the fundamentals of the situation. De Gaulle did not particularly like Britain but he understood us quite well. And perhaps because he was less of a Euro-idealist and more of a nationalist than Macmillan, he perceived where divergent national destinies should lead. As he now told the British Prime

Minister, he was 'against an integrated Europe; this was neither practicable, sensible, nor desirable, and the result would be a materialist, soulless mass, with no idealism left ... [T]he national identity of the European nations should be preserved'. And within such a framework of nation states Britain would always be the odd man out. As de Gaulle put it in the course of the famous press conference in January 1963 at which he explained his renewed 'Non' to British entry:

> England is ... insular, maritime, linked through its trade, markets, and food supply to very diverse and often very distant countries. Its activities are essentially industrial and commercial, and only slightly agricultural. It has ... very marked and original customs and traditions. In short, the nature, structure and economic context of England differ profoundly from those of the other States of the Continent ... It is foreseeable that the cohesion of all its members, who would be very numerous and very diverse, would not hold for long and that in the end there would appear a colossal Atlantic Community under American dependence and leadership which would soon completely swallow up the European Community.[10]

De Gaulle was half right – and from Britain's point of view it was the more important half. By her history and her interests Britain is indeed a fundamentally different kind of nation state to those which are involved in 'building' Europe. One would have to add, as de Gaulle himself could not, that it was more than economics that was at issue here. It was Britain's long history of continuous constitutional development, the respect in which her institutions were held, the honesty of her politicians and the integrity of her judges, the fact that not since the Norman Conquest had she known occupation, and that neither Nazism nor communism had ever gained a grip on her political life – all these things marked Britain out from Continental Europe. But, I repeat, the General was right in so far as his pride allowed: Britain *is* different. That is why Britain is still repeatedly at odds with the other European countries, however determinedly cooperative British politicians wish to be.

De Gaulle was, however, wrong in another respect. He imagined that his own principled and patriotic, if sometimes wanton and cantankerous, defence of France's national interests would be matched by his successors. He sincerely believed in a *Europe des états*, a Europe of sovereign states. But federalism, not Gaullism, was the destination to which the Euro-train was bound.

France's veto of Britain's entry into the Common Market seemed a bitter blow at the time. Almost no one in Britain – even those who were somewhat sceptical of the benefits of entry – thought that de Gaulle was right. His action was just deemed childish, insulting and irrational. After the initial annoyance had subsided, the desire to join the Common Market again began to flourish with renewed vigour among the British political class. It could even be argued that if de Gaulle was so determined to keep us out, was that not proof of the beneficial consequences of being in? What did he know that previous British leaders had not? So it was that Harold Wilson's Labour government made a new application in 1967, which was again rejected by France.

I had become a Member of Parliament at the general election of 1959, so I was in a position to follow these events with an educated if not an expert interest. During the whole of this period, I fully shared the prevailing view that Britain's national interest – particularly our economic interest – required joining the EEC on the best available terms. I also thought that it was important to maintain our links with and obligations to the Commonwealth. As someone who had a warm regard for Reggie Maudling,[11] the architect of EFTA, I felt that the merits of that modest organisation were insufficiently appreciated. But I was still for membership of the Common Market.

Ted Heath, who beat Reggie Maudling to become leader of the Conservative Party in 1965, and for whom I voted, was a passionate Euro-enthusiast. Like Macmillan, but with greater zeal and perhaps less finesse, he had emerged from his experiences in the services in wartime convinced that European unity was vital for peace and prosperity. Once Ted was in charge of the party, and if he won a general election, it was certain that Britain would strive to join the European Common Market with greater determination than ever. And with the replacement of de Gaulle by President Georges Pompidou in 1969, entry suddenly became possible.

When Britain did actually join the European Economic Community in January 1973 I was a member of Cabinet, as Education Secretary. I continued to view the decision as necessary and right. It was clear to all of us that the conditions, particularly as regards fisheries and agriculture, could be criticised. But the wider economic benefits seemed to outweigh the drawbacks, and above all it was imperative to break through the European tariff wall so that our goods could be sold freely to the markets of the Six, with their 190 million consumers.

Yet the forces which would push Europe in a direction other than that which we hoped were in truth much stronger than we then believed. We were, I am afraid it now appears, a little naïve. There is all the less excuse because we were warned. In retrospect, Enoch Powell's assertions during these years that what was involved by entry into the Common Market was not ultimately a matter of economics but rather an unacceptable loss of sovereignty turned out to be absolutely right.[12]

The most important reason to support EEC entry was, as I have noted, access to European markets. In those days, before the Uruguay Round of trade negotiations in the 1980s and 1990s resulted in large worldwide tariff cuts, the European external tariffs averaged some 12 per cent. So exclusion from the European customs union represented a significant obstacle to British trade. By contrast, other benefits which, it was alleged, would also follow even then seemed more nebulous. It was, for example, argued that our industries would become more efficient as greater competition within the Market helped eradicate restrictive practices, and weakened trade union obstruction. In fact, these benefits did not materialise at all: indeed, Britain never had worse industrial relations than in the years immediately after our entry into the EEC.

Why was there, then, not more and better debate about the merits and drawbacks of entry? There are, I now think, three main reasons. First, as is clear from official documents released under the 'thirty year rule', such debate was considered irrelevant by those with direct responsibility for the negotiations. The basis on which Britain joined was that we could hope to change nothing in Europe: we just had to take what we were offered. In his account of the negotiations of 1970–72, the late Sir Con O'Neill wrote:

> … the whole of our negotiations were peripheral, accidental and secondary. The general movement of events in 1969 and 1970 revived the opportunity, and was much more important than the negotiations themselves. What mattered was to get into the

Community, and thereby restore our position at the centre of European affairs which, since 1958, we had lost. The negotiations were concerned only with the means of achieving this objective at an acceptable price. They therefore had to be concerned with the Community as we found it, as it happened to be. None of its policies was essential to us; many of them were objectionable.[13]

No doubt those involved behaved honourably by their own lights. But I have to say that such is not in my experience the best way to get a reasonable deal in Europe, or anywhere else for that matter.

Secondly, for all the reasons which had been reiterated since the late 1950s, there seemed no alternative to the EEC – neither the Commonwealth, nor EFTA, nor any other trading partner fitted the bill. In Britain there was, underlying this perception, a strange, largely self-induced sense of impotence and isolation. The country had lost its direction with its mission. Here, it seemed to many, was another chance to find our destiny and to affect the destinies of others.

And third, both in 1970–72 (the debates about entry) and in 1975 (when the referendum was held to decide whether Britain should stay or leave) a series of highly misleading statements were made about what was involved. It would be pleasant to avoid referring to what was said. But an unvarnished assessment makes that impossible. I would just quote three instances:

There will not be a blueprint for a federal Europe ... What is more, those members of the Community who want a federal system, but who know the views of Her Majesty's Government and the Opposition parties here, are prepared to forgo their federal desires so that Britain should be a member.[14]

The Community is no federation of provinces or counties. It constitutes a Community of great and established nations, each with its own personality and traditions ... There is no question of any erosion of essential national sovereignty ... All the countries concerned recognise that an attempt to impose a majority view in a case where one or more members considered their vital national interests to be at stake would imperil the very fabric of the Community.[15]

There was a threat to employment in Britain from the movement in the Common Market towards an Economic and Monetary Union. This could have forced us to accept fixed exchange rates for the pound, restricting industrial growth and so putting jobs at risk. This threat has been removed.[16]

Each of these assertions has since turned out to be untrue, for reasons that I have described at some length in the previous chapter. Whether those who made these statements believed them to be true at the time I do not know.

Elsewhere I have set out in detail my own dealings with the European Community as Britain's Prime Minister between 1979 and 1990.[17] Here I shall simply reflect on the main issues and their significance.

The terms on which Britain joined the EEC were soon understood to have been unsatisfactory in a number of respects. That understanding – and the unhealed splits in Labour's ranks on the principle of Common Market membership – was why

James Callaghan's Labour government sought to 'renegotiate' the terms of Britain's membership prior to putting these to a referendum. In fact, renegotiation secured nothing of note, and not one penny piece reduction in Britain's exorbitant financial contributions. By the time I became Prime Minister in 1979, Britain was losing out across the board.

When I entered Downing Street, Britain was indeed on the verge of becoming the EEC's largest net contributor, even though we were then only the seventh richest nation per head. After several years of bruising negotiations, during which every device of procrastination and obfuscation was employed by our partners, I succeeded at the Fontainebleau summit in 1984 in having Britain's contributions substantially and permanently reduced. We were to receive back as a rebate roughly one-third of our net contributions, and that arrangement was to continue, as it still does. The cumulative value of that rebate between 1985 and 2000 amounted to more than £28 billion.[18]

This prolonged struggle for a fairer deal for Britain taught me a good deal about the EEC, most of it unflattering. But, odd as it may seem to my critics and even in retrospect to me, I still remained something of a European idealist. I really did believe that the sort of tough talking and hard negotiating which I had practised since 1979 could sharply reduce, if not actually eliminate, the weaknesses which held Europe back, and that it might be possible to shape an agenda that would see it become a force for economic progress. Thus the middle period of my time as Prime Minister, broadly 1984 to 1988, was heavily taken up with the development and implementation of the European Single Market.

The Single Market was very much a British initiative, though that is not to say that others, with varying motives, were not also keen. Its aim was to fulfil, as we in Britain saw it, the original goals of the Treaty of Rome, which I described at this time as a treaty for 'economic liberty'. The Single Market programme would achieve this by removing 'non-tariff barriers'. These operated, for example, through different national standards on health and safety, regulations and public procurement policies which discriminated against foreign products, and over-elaborate customs procedures.

It was hoped that their elimination would provide a general boost to intra-European trade, growth and employment. Some rather ambitious figures for each were widely floated. The European Commission's Cecchini Report predicted a one-off gain of 5 per cent to Europe's GNP (with an annual increase of 1 per cent thereafter), and 5.5 million more jobs in the longer term.[19] These projections, however, based as they were upon estimated effects of wider competition and economies of scale, were bound to be speculative.

More important, at least as far as I was concerned, were the potential gains for Britain. With our strength in services, and since we already enjoyed a lighter and more transparent system of regulation than our European competitors, the British economy, it was expected, would specially benefit.

The Single Market programme involved some 280 measures designed to harmonise standards and specification and thus open up markets. In order to see that this ambitious undertaking took effect during the five-year implementation period, we accepted a significant increase in majority voting within the Community. Without this, the programme itself could not have been driven through in the face of vested interests in member countries whose governments would have been under immense pressure to use the veto.

Britain was the originator of and continued to be the driving force behind the Single Market. But I had at first hoped to avoid a new inter-governmental conference to draw up a new treaty – an occasion which I well understood might be used to cause all sorts of mischief. It was only when it was clear that the other EEC members were intent on one that I accepted that there was no other way to bring them fully on board. Even then, I sought to do everything I could to ensure that the extra powers being given to the European Commission were not misused either to pile on regulation or to threaten vital national interests. Thus a 'general statement' was solemnly made at the Luxembourg Council, at which the terms of the Single European Act were agreed, stating:

> Nothing in these provisions shall affect the right of
> member states to take such measures as they consider
> necessary for the purpose of controlling immigration
> from third countries, and to combat terrorism, crime,
> the traffic in drugs and illicit trading in works of art and
> antiques.[20]

The Single European Act can now be assessed with the benefit of a decade's hindsight, and since others have made their – often critical – assessments, I should now add mine. The first question is: did the Single Market programme achieve the economic benefits for which we hoped? On this the experts still differ.[21] The main difficulty, of course, in making a firm judgement arises from the inescapable weakness in all such hypothetical analyses, namely that we cannot know what might have occurred *without* the Single Market programme. But it seems clear that a good deal of the optimism has proved unfounded.

On the one hand, the Single Market programme may have worked with other independent, global factors to widen competition and open markets. But on the other, the process of harmonisation clearly also resulted in many cases in more harmful regulation – as has been exposed by that indefatigable campaigner against bureaucratic imbecilities, Christopher Booker.[22] The importance of this can only be grasped if we recall that, in principle, the new regulations affect the whole of the British economy, not just firms involved in exporting to the EEC. And only 15.5 per cent of Britain's total GDP consists of such exports.[23] For those firms that are either entirely involved with the domestic market or those doing business with non-EEC countries extra regulation is all loss and no corresponding gain.

In any case, and most seriously, I believe that in negotiating the Single European Act we in Britain made two understandable but undeniable mistakes. The first was to assume that the increased powers given to the Commission would cease to be used to any great extent once the Single Market programme had been completed. After all, if one accepted that the whole purpose of the changes made was to establish a properly functioning market, there was no reason to imagine that the process would be anything other than finite. True, one could not hand back vetoes that had been removed as part of the Single European Act, because governments might subvert the progress that had been made. But there was no reason to think the Commission would need to keep legislating at the same rate, let alone spread its legislative tentacles more widely.

The aim was said to be a 'level playing field'. This phrase has a reassuring ring to it, but it actually encapsulates a fundamental error about trade. Free trade allows firms in differing nations to compete. But because a 'level playing field' stops that part of competition that comes from differing regulative systems it actually reduces the gains from trade. Moreover, as every British schoolboy knows, levelling playing fields does not involve the removal of every minor lump, bump and worm-cast. At some point the reshaping and rolling, the raising and lowering, have to stop so that the game itself can continue normally. This perception, rather obvious to those of us who understood the realities of enterprise, unfortunately proved difficult for Europe's bureaucratic utopians to grasp.

The second error, which was closely linked to the first, was then and later to take at face value the assurances we were given. I do not now believe that the European Commission or the majority of European governments were ever much interested in economics. They viewed, and still view, policy as equivalent to politics, and politics as about power – and only power. The Single Market thus appealed to these forces, which were already increasingly in the ascendant despite my successes with Britain's rebate, as a device for centralising more decision-making in the hands of Europe. And the idea that these extra powers should be limited to the purpose for which they were actually being given probably never seriously occurred to them.

The European Commission and the European Court of Justice worked together to explore, exploit and widen every loophole. And as they did so, they could rely on the support of most of the member countries and the European Parliament which both shared the federalist dream and were deeply committed to achieving that European social and economic model which I have described at some length in the previous chapter. Indeed, the drive for a 'Social Europe', so beloved of Jacques Delors,[24] then President of the European Commission and the man who must above all be credited (or blamed) for what has occurred, soon adopted at least as much importance as the 'Economic Europe' which the Single Market sought to create.

Thus the provisions of the Single European Act were abused in order to push corporatist and collectivist social legislation upon Britain by the back door. For example, the Working Time Directive was introduced by the Commission under Article 118a, a health and safety provision which had been inserted into the Treaty of Rome by the Single European Act. Classing the Directive as a health and safety instead of a social measure meant that it could be pushed through under qualified majority voting (QMV), bypassing Britain's veto. This stratagem was then upheld by the European Court in 1996. Such measures may sound innocuous, indeed attractive, in themselves. But they represent an unwelcome interference in Britain's affairs, and the underlying purpose is obvious – it is to reduce Britain's ability to compete successfully. Now that the Labour government has misguidedly signed up to the European Social Chapter we can expect much more of this.

Of the phrase 'Single European Market', it has thus turned out that the first two words drained a good deal of the substance from the third. Mutual recognition of standards, and indeed the setting in some cases of a minimum standard, are acceptable, *as long as* they genuinely make trade easier. But if harmonisation goes beyond this, it is merely costly, bureaucratic and illiberal. Above all, if harmonisation is taken beyond technical standards and the like, and is also applied to labour laws, social security and taxation, it is profoundly economically destructive. This is because competition between different countries to provide the most conducive international conditions for enterprise is a powerful engine of economic advance. Once smother that competition, and European governments will have no hesitation in imposing ever-increasing burdens. The result will inevitably be a flight of capital and talent to non-European countries. And on top of all that, of course, is the unacceptable frustration of democracy when an unaccountable supra-national authority decides matters which properly fall to national governments. So, given all these considerations – and given the fact that global forces for free trade have actually proved stronger than those operating within Europe – I cannot rate the European Single Act as other than a disappointment. History does not allow us to retrace our steps. But it does allow us and our successors to learn from what has transpired. This we should now do.

Already towards the end of my time as Prime Minister I was becoming increasingly concerned at the way Single Market measures were being used to impose socialist-style regulation by the back door. It was clear to me that in the struggle to liberalise and decentralise the European Community Britain was fighting a lone and perhaps unwinnable battle. One could forge short-term tactical alliances with other states on particular measures, but Britain alone was exclusively interested in making of the Community an enterprise-friendly common market: the others had different priorities. In the end one had to be unafraid of isolation and simply say 'no'. Of course, that strategy required sufficient political will and sufficient political support from my party: in the event, however, the latter was not forthcoming.

My departure from office ensured that the path to federalism could be trodden more smoothly and swiftly. And so it has been. Under my successor, whose hope it was to place Britain at the 'heart of Europe', the Maastricht Treaty was signed in February 1992. Although this secured Britain an opt-out from the single currency, it also allowed that fraught enterprise to go forward elsewhere. It established a European citizenship and a common defence policy, 'which might lead in time to a common defence'. It also established a 'Committee of the

Regions', which marked a complementary approach of trying to undermine the sovereignty of nation states from below. And although Britain opted out of the Social Chapter, as I have already noted above that did not in fact prevent the European Commission from trying with some success to impose higher social costs on Britain.

Britain's attitude towards the European project has, therefore, altered much over the years, depending upon the politics of governments and the personalities of Prime Ministers. And indeed the European issue will, and must, remain one upon which the main political parties offer contrasting approaches. Yet looking back over the years since Britain became a member of the EEC in 1973, I am struck by what all these British governments, including mine, had in common. And this is perhaps as significant as the more obvious differences.

It may sound trite, but it is also true that all of us were doing our best, as we saw it from differing angles, to serve British national interests in Europe. And yet none of us was able to do more than partially improve the otherwise unfavourable terms of our membership – if that.

In 1972 Ted Heath conceded control over our fish stocks, acceptance of an appallingly wasteful CAP and excessive financial contributions in exchange for wider economic objectives. But the gain never materialised, and the pain did.

For my part, I secured a fundamental renegotiation of our financial contributions to Europe, thus righting one major problem which Ted and Jim Callaghan after him had failed to resolve. But Britain continued and continues to bear an unfair and excessive financial burden. Pressure to reform the CAP and Europe's finances had only limited success. The one positive attempt which Britain made to make the European Community market-friendly, the Single Market, was eventually largely hijacked by the European bureaucracy. And Britain's partners then forced upon Europe an agenda of economic and monetary union against our strongly expressed wishes.

John Major, partly because of his personality and partly because of the circumstances under which he became Prime Minister, tried to defend Britain's interests through gaining special exemptions – on the single currency and the Social Chapter – rather than by holding up in principle the march to federalism, of which I think he probably disapproved. Yet the European Commission relentlessly and successfully pressed unwelcome regulations upon British industry. And the victory that John thought he had won at Maastricht through gaining support for the principle of 'subsidiarity' – which holds that nothing should be decided by an upper tier of authority that can adequately be decided by a lower one – has not actually led to Europe relinquishing one single power to national governments. Nor will it. Another betrayal.

Even Tony Blair's determinedly Euro-enthusiastic New Labour government has found that its attempts to trade on European 'good will' have all been in vain. It is still under siege on the issue of tax harmonisation – notably VAT rates, company taxation and fuel taxes. Problems lie ahead too on labour market regulation and border controls. The attempt to burnish the Blair government's European credentials by signing up to a European defence force has been used by the French to pursue their own anti-American agenda, jeopardising Mr Blair's – I believe genuine – desire to see Britain remain a dependable ally of the United States.

Reviewing all these experiences, we can see that any concessions which Britain makes, or initiatives which she promotes, in Europe are always eventually turned against her and against the original intention. The style, tone and temperament of

EU MEMBERS, EU CANDIDATE STATES AND NON-EU MEMBERS, 2002

0
0   600 km

ICELAND
• Reykjavik

NORWAY
Oslo •

■ EU states
■ EU candidate states

North
Sea

DENMARK

NETHERLANDS
BELGIUM

IRELAND   Dublin

BRITAIN
London •

The Hague

GERMA

Brussles •

GERMA

Paris •   LUXEMBOURG

Atlantic Ocean

• Bern

SWITZERLAND

FRANCE   ITALY

SLOV

SPAIN

Rom

PORTUGAL

Madrid •

Mediterranean
Sea

Lisbon •

British governments may change. But attempts to find a *modus vivendi* with Europe in any major policy area always fail sooner or later. Only credible threats of disruption – like mine in the early 1980s – yield results. And these, though they can secure important gains, are still unable to shift the direction in which Europe as a whole is going.

Moreover – and this is the crucial point now – as more and more powers pass from nation states to Brussels, it becomes steadily more difficult to deflect or veto those new measures which harm our interests. Thus over the years the number of measures subject to QMV rather than unanimity has steadily grown. Nor is this the only difficulty, for even as regards measures introduced under QMV our ability to construct a blocking minority is diminishing.[25] And as for the so-called Luxembourg Compromise – the understanding that if a country declared that its national interests were fundamentally at stake its veto would stand – that has now, it seems, passed entirely into oblivion.[26]

In recent years the Conservative Party's approach has been summarised in the slogan 'In Europe, but not run by Europe'. That is fair enough as an aspiration. But is it an available option? And if not, where does that leave us? The need now, with the 2001 general election behind us, is for a fresh look at policy towards Europe on a realistic basis, without having recourse either to wishful thinking or to slogans.

KEEP THE POUND

The first priority, though, is to avoid making matters worse. And abolishing sterling to replace it with the euro would make them much worse. The Conservative Party was right to pledge to keep the pound at the last election. But it was judged appropriate to limit that promise only to the duration of a parliament.

Unfortunately, while perfectly satisfactory in practice – no one seriously thought that a Conservative government led by William Hague would give up the pound – the limited pledge was not very logical. The principal arguments against Britain's joining the European single currency are not, after all, dependent on circumstances: they depend, rather, on matters of fundamental belief which cannot be glossed over or minimised if Conservatives wish to be taken seriously. An illogical compromise on this occasion got the Conservative Party – as in 1997 – into trouble on something which should have been a vital source of strength and support. Unnecessary opportunities were provided for the party's opponents to highlight divisions; the tiny pro-euro minority in the party were not appeased; and votes were lost to the UK Independence Party, which was thought to take a clearer and more principled stand. One can argue about the different possible lessons to be drawn from the election campaign and its outcome. But there is no argument for continuing timidity on the score of the single currency. The Conservative Party should go into any future election pledged to keep the pound sterling – just as it is pledged to keep our freedom and our sovereignty – for good. It can never be right for Britain to abolish its currency. And it can never be right for the Conservative Party to pretend otherwise.[27]

The reason why that is so is, for a British patriot, self-evident. As I have sought to demonstrate, the power to issue and control one's own currency is a fundamental aspect of sovereignty. Sovereignty is a necessary, though not sufficient, condition for freedom and democracy. It is not sufficient, because a government which exercises authority over a nation may, of course, be or become tyrannical or at least authoritarian. But sovereignty is a necessary condition, because unless a government truly has the authority and power to govern – unless it really *is a govern-*

ment – the constitution cannot be upheld and the democratic mandate becomes a nonsense.

Sometimes arguments about sovereignty are stretched and distorted in such labyrinthine fashion that one would need to be a genius to understand them.[28] But it is clear that, alongside the other transfers of power which have taken and are taking place, our transfer to the European Union of the authority to issue currency would move us a long way towards losing our sovereignty. It would, moreover, do this in a way which struck a body blow at our democracy. I made this point in an article which appeared during the May/June 2001 general election campaign:

> Without its own currency, Britain would lose the power to determine its own economic policy … There is nothing very complicated about what is at stake. With a single currency, there would be a single interest rate, set not to take account of Britain's needs, but those of a range of different countries – a recipe for 'boom and bust' indeed.[29] And there would be immense and, in the end, irresistible pressure to allow our budgets to be made by Europe as well. Indeed, with the so-called 'Stability Pact', which limits budget deficits, and with progressive harmonisation of taxes, the direction is already evident.
>
> Add to that the social regulation that will come from Brussels under whatever provision the Commission thinks it can abuse, and the result is clear. The main issues relating to Britain's economic well-being would be removed from Britain's control. And yet it is about these very issues that every British election in modern times has been fought.[30]

The abolition of sterling would not, it should be remembered, be merely equivalent to setting up a currency board, by which a country chooses to link its own currency to another, such as the US dollar. It may decide to do this for a variety of reasons – for example, because it wishes to bolster confidence in its anti-inflation strategy, or simply because it does so much trade with the country against whose currency its own is fixed. But such arrangements, however much politicians and bankers may pretend otherwise, are limited. They are entered into voluntarily: voluntarily, too, they can be ended.

By contrast, the Maastricht Treaty, which instituted the European single currency, contains no provision for withdrawal from it. The European Commission President, Romano Prodi, has seemed to suggest that a country could abolish its currency and then, if it changed its mind about the euro, start to issue it again.[31] In view of the wording of the protocol in the Maastricht Treaty which declares 'the irreversible character of the Community's movement to the third stage of Economic and Monetary Union', this is rather odd. But if Signor Prodi actually knew what he was saying, then he was being disingenuous. Of course it is open to any European country at any stage to declare UDI from the Union or to pull out of the euro. In the case of Britain, as I shall explain, our traditional constitutional doctrine indeed holds that that power can never ultimately be abandoned or lost by our Parliament. But the financial and technical obstacles involved in reissuing a national currency after one's reserves had been transferred to the European Central Bank and one's own central bank had acquired the status of an ECB branch office would be daunting. The then European Commissioner for EMU, Yves-Thibault de Silguy, expressed the commonly accepted view when he bluntly said: 'There is no provision in the treaty for a country which has joined monetary union subsequently to leave. There are no procedures for going backwards. That is why you have to be certain when you join up.'[32]

I am certain. We should not join.

So there are strong reasons in principle – political and constitutional reasons – why Britain should stay out of the euro. But there are plenty of practical economic reasons too. Not the least of these is Britain's experience when sterling was part of the European Exchange Rate Mechanism (ERM). Shadowing the Deutschmark from March 1987, what might be called sterling's 'informal' (and by me unauthorised) ERM policy, was responsible for keeping interest rates too low, which in turn allowed inflation to rise. Sterling formally joined the ERM in October 1990, a month before my departure from Downing Street. But I made clear that it was upon monetary policy, based upon assessment of domestic monetary conditions, that we would primarily rely when setting interest rates.[33]

This subsequently changed. The ERM was now treated as the Europeans themselves had always viewed it, namely as a prelude to economic and monetary union. Maintaining a particular parity of exchange rate took precedence over all other economic considerations. This rigidity was disastrous. When German interest rates rose because of borrowing to cover the costs of East German reunification, those high interest rates were passed on through the mechanism of the ERM to us, for whom they deepened and lengthened the recession. Finally, on Black (or arguably, White) Wednesday (16 September 1992), after some £11 billion of reserves had been spent, and after interest rates had risen to 12 per cent (with 15 per cent announced for the following day), sterling had to withdraw from the ERM. Contrary to the dire warnings received, the pound did not collapse. And far from collapsing, the economy began to recover, even if the then Conservative government's reputation for economic competence did not.

If Britain had been part of EMU at the time, the effects on our economy would have been still more serious because the straitjacket would have been still tighter. There would have been no way to relieve the pressure on British industry by dropping interest rates and the value of the currency. We would have been locked fast into an over-restrictive monetary policy and an inappropriate exchange rate. Subsidies, or emigration, or real wage cuts would have been the only (and deeply unsatisfactory) policy options available to try to cope with worsening recession. What government would have welcomed that? These are matters upon which the dwindling minority of British enthusiasts for the abolition of sterling in favour of the euro should reflect.

There can never, in truth, be a 'right' interest rate, or indeed a 'right' exchange rate, for the whole of Europe. The economies of the European countries are simply too diverse. But over and above that there are also particular difficulties for Britain, whose economy is fundamentally dissimilar to those of most of our neighbours.

The British economy is, and for the foreseeable future will remain, much more sensitive to interest rate changes than the economies of mainland Europe. This is because we, unlike them, have a high level of variable mortgage debt due to our traditional emphasis on home ownership. A further reason for suggesting that Britain is economically different lies in the fact that our business cycle does not generally follow that on the Continent: it is far more closely in harmony with that in the United States. Unlike Europe, Britain is a major oil producer. We are also much more dependent than the Europeans on so-called 'invisible earnings', that is services and investment income. Finally, because – as I shall examine later – so much of our trade is with non-European countries and thus not denominated in euros at all, we would have less to gain from removing the costs arising from exchange-rate volatility against the euro. Indeed, locking our exchange rate into Europe's would actually increase the pound's volatility against the dollar, with which sterling has usually moved. And, finally, in answer to those who say that they want a common currency easily available for use throughout the world, this already exists – it is called the US dollar.

The euro is not necessary for Britain to prosper. Participation in a single currency is not necessary for free trade: the North American Free Trade Area (NAFTA), comprising the US, Canada and Mexico, works perfectly well (and, as I shall show, better than the EU) without one. But the euro could certainly harm global free trade, which in turn would disproportionately hurt Britain, in so far as the single currency locked in higher costs and so fuelled Europe's inherent protectionism. Contrary to the gloomy predictions made when it was launched, we can now see clearly that the euro is not necessary for the City of London to thrive: since the euro was born the City has dominated the euro trade and flourished mightily. This is mainly because of the City of London's unmatched skills and its global reputation – and also because of a business-friendly tax and regulatory regime, which exists in Britain despite, not because of, the EU. Finally, the European single currency is not necessary either to attract inward investment to Britain. In 1999 Britain was the most popular destination in the EU for foreign direct investment, with its share rising from 25 per cent to 27 per cent, double that of France and nearly three times that of Germany.[34] Foreigners invest here because the costs which Britain imposes on business are low, and notably lower than in mainland Europe – hence indignant French protests at so-called 'social dumping'.

INTERNATIONAL LABOUR COSTS
Social Insurance expenditures and other labour taxes as a percentage of hourly compensation costs for production workers in manufacturing, 1999

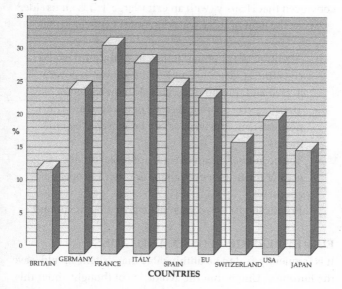

Source: U.S. Bureau of Labor Statistics

Abolishing the pound and substituting the euro would be enormously disruptive. It would also be extremely costly – the one-off costs to Britain have been estimated as between £31 billion and £35 billion.[35] Indeed, prematurely and wastefully, the British government has already embarked upon a programme to 'prepare' British industry for a change-over which the great majority of the British public do not want to see at all. Opinion polls suggest that some 65 to 70 per cent are opposed.[36] Not that this appears to affect the intentions of the political-bureaucratic elite, which in Britain as elsewhere in Europe believes that it has an overriding mission to achieve European integration by hook or by crook and which is convinced that History (with an extra-large 'H') is on its side.[37]

So, in the light of these considerations, I conclude that:

- Abolition of the pound in favour of the euro would constitute a major loss of Britain's power to govern herself and thus an unacceptable blow to democracy
- The alleged economic benefits of the euro are either non-existent, or trivial, or can be achieved by other means
- The economic disadvantages are substantially greater for Britain even than for other European countries
- Britain should not contemplate giving up the pound.

EU MEMBERSHIP – LOSSES AND GAINS

It is frequently said to be unthinkable that Britain should leave the European Union. But the avoidance of thought about this, as about other matters, is a poor substitute for judgement. It is only when we honestly weigh up the losses and gains that we can decide which is the sensible course.

A good deal of probably well-intentioned pressure has been exerted in order to prevent this issue being raised at all, at least before any referendum on Britain's joining the euro. I understand why many opponents of EMU feel that that would be the prudent course. They know, as do the proponents of the euro, what the opinion polls show – namely that while a substantial majority of the British public oppose losing the pound, only a large minority at present favour leaving the EU altogether.[38] The Euro-enthusiasts recognise that probably their only hope of winning a referendum on the euro is to fight it as if it were really a referendum on EU membership. They evidently plan a re-run of the alarmist tactics of 1975, when a large majority voted to remain within the EEC.

This, of course, is dishonest nonsense. Whatever EU Commissioners or Euro-enthusiast politicians may threaten, it is clear that Britain's rights as an EU member, established under the various EU treaties, are unaffected by any decision to stay out of the single currency. There is another factor which the Euro-enthusiasts should consider rather seriously. If they insist on using the argument that rejecting the euro means rejecting Europe as such, then they could find themselves in a very awkward position indeed if the vote went against them. It would widely and with much justification be taken as a mandate for a fundamental renegotiation of Britain's position in the EU, not excluding the option of unilateral withdrawal. I would welcome that approach. But would they? Empty warnings of imminent doom can suddenly become self-fulfilling. I am sure that the story of the little boy who cried 'Wolf!', only then to become the latter's breakfast, must be available in translation in many European languages.

But, of course, there is one thing to be said for what the alarmists allege, though again I doubt it would please them to acknowledge it. The concept of the euro is indeed the clearest expression that we have so far of the direction in which those in charge of Europe want to go – namely, towards a federal superstate. The European single currency is intended to take its place alongside a European legal system, a European foreign policy, a European army, a European Parliament and a European government to create a European superstate. In this sense, the debate about the euro is part and parcel of a growing, necessary and overdue debate about Britain's attitude towards a European Union which is rapidly evolving into something more than a mere Union.

So I return to my starting point. Let us in Britain at last really *think* about what we expect from Europe as it is presently constituted, calculate whether we are getting it, and, if not, consider whether we could do better creating some new trading arrangement.

There have been a number of attempts to work out a 'balance sheet' of losses and gains from Britain's EU membership. The calculation changes, of course, as the EU itself acquires new powers and as conditions alter in the world outside Europe. It is also easier to establish the narrower financial than the broader economic picture.

Even after the rebates which I secured in the mid-1980s, Britain is a large net contributor to the EU budget. In 2000 the figure stood at £2.4 billion. Since we joined the EEC, our net contribution has amounted to £54.7 billion. But it is not enough to look at the net contribution, that is what we pay less what we receive. It is the gross contribution – amounting to £5.9 billion in 2000 alone – which is also important, because this sum represents public expenditure which is in large measure spent on other things than a British government and British electors would choose.[39] Incidentally, it is really quite remarkable how easily this point is lost and becomes submerged in barrages of misleading figures about how much different regions and local-es of the United Kingdom 'receive' from Europe. I agree with former Chancellor of the Exchequer, Norman (now Lord) nt, who has noted that this 'is a bit like the campaign slogan of the Mayor of Sao Paolo in Brazil who said: "I steal, but I give some back."[40]

The reason why Britain loses out financially from Europe is now – as ever – the CAP. The CAP leads to bureaucracy and to poor use of our natural resources. But its most damaging impact is that upon the wider economy, by forcing up food prices – something which is particularly damaging for an advanced, urbanised country like Britain.

Like the other economic effects of EU membership, that of the CAP is, though, difficult to calculate. One cannot, for example, simply compare food prices within the EU and those on the world market and say that the difference is the extra we pay. This is because world prices are lower than they would otherwise be because the EU dumps the produce which it has over-produced on to world markets. However, Patrick Minford estimates that the cost of the CAP for a typical year would be some £6.5 billion. This is based upon taking the cost to consumers of paying higher prices for food, subtracting the gain to British farmers, and then adding the loss in real income from reduced consumption of food. The figure rises to £15 billion (roughly 1.5 per cent of GDP) if the UK's net budgetary contribution to the EEC to support the CAP's deficit and running costs is added.[41]

The costs and benefits for Britain of EU membership across the board are still more difficult to estimate. For example, do we assume that free trade with EU member countries is a benefit inseparable from EU membership? Or could we negotiate favourable terms of access to those markets from outside? (I shall examine this option later.) Again, though to non-economists this may seem counter-intuitive, there will be some economic *cost* to Britain through being within the European tariff wall. As with the old system of Imperial

Preference, privileged access to protected markets, though it may initially be attractive, has the effect of damaging the global competitiveness of one's industries.[42] But the EU tariff wall is, in any case, now quite low: so the balance of advantage and disadvantage in respect of trade is fairly evenly matched and not very significant.

Where does this leave the balance sheet? On the one hand, in what seems to me a 'worst case' scenario, an analysis by the National Institute of Economic and Social Research has concluded that 'the level of UK output would be about 2 per cent per annum lower outside the EU than inside'. It argues that some jobs would be lost, but adds that 'there is no reason to suppose that the UK will experience mass unemployment outside the EU'. The NIESR accepts that 'outside the EU the UK could take advantage of lower world food prices and could benefit from savings on its contributions to the EU budget'. But it believes that 'these effects would be outweighed by the effects of higher tariffs and administrative costs on exports and by a resulting fall in the number of firms investing in the UK'.[43]

Although the study emphasises the alleged disadvantages of exit from the EU, it also disproves the economically illiterate and socially alarmist warnings from, for example, Keith Vaz, then Minister for Europe, that 3.5 million jobs would be lost if we left the European Union.[44] I doubt the NIESR's other conclusions, though, because I do not think that it is realistic to suppose that we would be unable to negotiate any special trade relationship with the EU. I do not think either that there would be an adverse effect on investment in Britain, and the NIESR's judgement is heavily influenced by that.[45] Foreign investors are, evidence suggests, a good deal more concerned about our costs, rather than the mere fact of EU market access, and since we could be even more successful in keeping costs down outside than inside the EU I would expect more not less inward investment. I think, too, that it is unlikely that we would subsidise farming to the same level if we were not part of the CAP. And the fall in the price of food imports – which the NIESR estimates at 20 per cent – could well be greater.

Patrick Minford's judgement, made in 1996 – that is *before* a Labour government signed Britain up to the Social Chapter and pledged to try to take Britain into EMU – seems to me more soundly based: 'There is no balance of advantage to speak of for or against our European membership. It makes sense to try and make a success of that membership, as so much has been invested in it. But in spite of all our efforts if our partners will not tolerate the conditions for that success, then we can walk away in confidence.'[46]

There are, though, those who think that the arguments for Britain's membership of the EU are not to be addressed in such matter-of-fact terms. Perhaps because I was a shopkeeper's daughter, or perhaps just because as Prime Minister I developed a preference for matters of fact, I cannot agree. If we are receiving an unsatisfactory deal and we have no realistic chance of improving it, and if at the same time we are steadily losing our powers of self-government, that seems sufficient argument against further integration in Europe for me.

I am not, for example, at all impressed by the suggestion that Britain is taken more seriously because we are part of a wider European whole. This view is mistaken because it rests on three fundamental errors.

First, it assumes that the exertion of 'influence', or indeed power, is an end in itself. It isn't. The possibility that Britain might be more successful in bossing other countries around if tied into a multinational colossus is a deeply unappealing, and of course profoundly illiberal, argument for integration with

Europe. To be free is better than to be unfree – always. Any politician who suggests the opposite should be treated as suspect.

Second, those who hold this view make an assumption of a necessary and absolute compatibility between the interests of Britain and those of the other countries of Europe. Again, this is simply not true. As I have already sought to demonstrate, Britain really is 'different'. Actually, I believe that if they were willing to investigate the matter honestly and intelligently the politicians of Europe would discover that the interests of their nations were 'different' and conflicting in important ways too; but, of course, in euro-land that would be heresy, and the Euro-Inquisition would soon set political funeral pyres a-smoking. In any case, as de Gaulle realised, Britain's economic and geopolitical interests are unique and uniquely divergent from Europe's. To overlook that and to search instead for the lowest European common denominator is profoundly misguided.

Third, and last, it is highly questionable whether when 'Europe speaks with one voice', as we are so often told it is doing, anyone is really listening. Europe's reputation as a serious player in international affairs is unenviable. It is a feeble giant whose desperate attempts to be taken seriously are largely risible. It has a weak currency and a sluggish inflexible economy, still much reliant on hidden protectionism. It has a shrinking, ageing population and, with the exception of Britain, rather unimpressive armed forces and, not excepting Britain, muddled diplomacy. There are better ways of increasing the country's international standing than through a common European foreign and security policy, let alone common European defence.

OPTIONS

So what should we do? The obvious preference would be to try to retain as much as possible of the existing arrangements, while opting out of present and future mechanisms which harm our interests or restrict our freedom of action. Any sensible person would hope that this approach would yield results, particularly any sensible Conservative – after all, one traditional aspect of conservatism is the unwillingness to make unnecessary changes. I advocated a variant of it in, for example, a speech in The Hague in 1992:

> Why need every new European initiative require the participation of all members of the Community? It will sometimes be the case – especially after enlargement – that only some Community members will want to move ahead to another stage of integration …
>
> We should aim for a multi-track Europe in which *ad hoc* groups of different states – such as the Schengen Group – forge varying levels of cooperation and integration on a case-by-case basis. Such a structure would lack graph-paper neatness. But it would accommodate the diversity of post-communist Europe.[47]

By the time that I came to write at length about Europe, some three years later, I was still more concerned with the direction in which events were leading. I viewed the attempt, which was already mooted and which is again firmly on the agenda, to create a 'two tier' Europe (in which some countries, France, Germany and others, might integrate faster) as offering Britain an opportunity essentially to renegotiate some of our terms of membership. But this would require determination to see that any attempts to create a 'hard core' of countries respected

Britain's fundamental interests. So those countries must not be allowed to impose on other EU members their own priorities on questions like the operation of the Single Market. The price of Britain's agreement to treaty changes might, I argued, be the 'unbundling' of a number of provisions – like those relating to our budget contributions and the CAP – which currently worked to our disadvantage.[48]

Was this still a realistic option at the time when I put it forward? It is difficult to be sure. Maastricht was by then, of course, on the statute book, and it was already clear that the talk of its being a decentralising treaty was so much hot air. Moreover, Maastricht had provided the treaty basis for a single currency, even though Britain had an opt-out. Once the single currency went ahead, a huge new step towards European federalism would have occurred. At least, though, we still had a Conservative government, so whatever reservations I might have had about its robustness on European issues, I knew that it would remain under heavy pressure from within the party to hold out against federalism.

But I also began to advance an alternative approach, which sought a more fundamental change in our relationship with the EU in order to preserve or (depending upon your viewpoint) to restore Britain's legal sovereignty. Thus I argued for 'amending the 1972 European Communities Act to establish the ultimate supremacy of Parliament over all Community law, making clear that Parliament can by express provision override Community law'. Among other more detailed suggestions, I then called for 'a reserve list of protected matters where Parliament alone can legislate, to include our constitutional arrangements and defence'.[49]

I believe that, had they been heeded, these suggestions might have formed the basis for a full-scale renegotiation of our

terms of membership. But the Major government took a different view, and in any case it lacked a parliamentary majority to
give effect to any such approach.

There was a change of view when William Hague became
Conservative Party leader after the 1997 general election. He
understood the need for rethinking and, within what appeared
the limits of prudence, sought to practise it. But by then, of
course, the Conservative Party was out of power. Tony Blair's
Labour government brought with it to Downing Street a determination to take Britain further towards federalism. Thus
Britain accepted the Social Chapter, from which John Major
had secured an opt-out. Mr Blair declared his support in principle for the abolition of sterling in favour of the euro, though
leaving the timing vague. Most seriously of all, perhaps, Britain's
long-standing opposition to European defence integration was
replaced by support for it. The Amsterdam and Nice Treaties
eased the federalist project forward. And for the immediate
future Britain will have a government prepared to make further
sacrifices of sovereignty and rigidly opposed to any attempts to
regain it.

In these circumstances, and given the speed with which the
federalist project is now being driven in Brussels and the other
European capitals, it is no longer realistic to imagine that a
future Conservative government will be able to achieve its goals
for renegotiation while pledged to remain a member of the EU
under anything like the present arrangements. Even now, it
would require a sea change of opinion in France or Germany
– and then an unprecedented level of British diplomatic success
– to assemble an effective alliance to stop, or slow, let alone
reverse the momentum. And to suggest that in, say, five years'
time that will be possible is not credible. For these reasons, I do
not think that talk of 'variable geometry', 'tiers', 'tracks', 'flexibil-

ity clauses' and all the rest is any longer worth the effort. No one is likely to be convinced. And, all things considered, no one should be.

So where does that leave us in negotiating a better relationship with the other member states of the EU? Actually, rather well-placed. The blunt truth is that the rest of the European Union needs us more than we need them. It is just that we have managed to entangle ourselves with Europe in such a way that these strengths cannot at present be used effectively.

Just consider the following three negotiating advantages which we enjoy. First, we are substantial net importers from the rest of the EU – to the tune of $16 billion in 1998.[50] As a free trader, I understand that trade is not to be considered a zero-sum activity. Trade benefits all who participate in it. But the fact remains that those European imports into Britain are of enormous importance to European companies and their workforces. Many thousands of European jobs depend on them. If we were to seek to change our trading relations with the EU, no matter how ill-tempered EU politicians might become, EU workers are going to bring pressure on them to keep our markets open. And that in turn means keeping Europe's markets open too.[51] Europe cannot afford a trade war with Britain – even if the WTO were ever to allow one.

Second, Europe will continue to want access to our waters and our fish. We are, as I have described, substantial contributors to the CAP, and the prospect of an end to that bounty might send our partners into a lather. But they have gained one other benefit from the terms of our entry which, to a number of them – particularly Spain – is extremely economically important, namely access to our fish stocks.

Perhaps the worst single aspect of the deal Britain made on entering the EEC related to fishing. Under measures which were dreamt up at the last moment by the Six in order to gain control over the fish of the four applicant countries – Britain, Norway, Ireland and Denmark – the Europeans resolved to regard fish as a 'common resource' to which all member states would have equal access. (The Norwegians were sufficiently angry about this to reject entry as a result in 1972 and again in 1994, and have prospered greatly since – the country now has the third highest GDP per head in Europe.) A few years later, national fishing limits were extended under international law from twelve to two hundred miles. Once Spain with its huge fishing fleet joined the EEC, and once the ten-year transitional period came to an end, the full implications of all this for Britain were unpleasantly apparent. There was massive over-fishing, and European attempts at conservation were ineffectual. Indeed, they did more harm than good when an absurd system of quotas forced large quantities of dead fish to be thrown back into the sea with damaging environmental consequences. The British fishing fleet shrank drastically – the number of British deep-sea fishing vessels has fallen from several hundred to just fourteen – and the inroads of Spanish fishermen were legitimised in the courts against the express wishes of the British Parliament.[52]

This cannot be allowed to continue. If Britain were to exert its parliamentary sovereignty and take back control of its waters within the two-hundred-mile limit, there would be an outcry in Brussels – but we would be quite within our rights and we could then regulate entry by bilateral agreement with other countries. This would not only establish an effective means of conservation by the exercise of national sovereignty – for it is an old truth that where no one owns no one cares – it would also ensure that all those European countries which wanted to fish in British waters, from which up to 80 per cent of 'Europe's' fish are taken, would suddenly become very cooperative on this, and indeed on other matters.

Third, however much the Europeans huff and puff about a common European foreign and security policy and a common defence, they know perfectly well that Britain as a European power is in a league of her own. Our language, our links through trade and political influence, our outlook, our closeness with America, our nuclear deterrent – all make us a global power, though not of course a superpower. Not even France, which comes nearest, is any longer a global force in the sense that this is true of Britain. If the EU is to become a global power itself (as it intends) it will need to have cooperative relations with Britain. We may even be called upon to pull its 'rapid reaction' forces out of ill-considered scrapes that arise from an excess of hubris and a lack of advanced weaponry.

Against this background, we should have every confidence that we can achieve a sensible framework within which to defend and pursue our interests – while having cooperative relations with the European countries. How might this be done?

The preliminary step, I believe, should be for an incoming Conservative government to declare publicly that it seeks fundamental renegotiation of Britain's terms of EU membership. The objectives would need to be set out clearly in a White Paper. There would be five.

First, from Britain's point of view, no satisfactory relationship is possible with the rest of Europe which sees us remaining subject to the CAP. Withdrawing from that system would mean both an end to the problem of our net contributions and gaining access to cheaper food imports – both highly desirable and extremely popular. We could at the same time establish a system of support for our agriculture which was environmentally sensitive and suitable for our own particular conditions.

Second, we have also, as I have noted above, to end our adherence to the Common Fisheries Policy. We would establish arrangements for sensible exploitation of our fish stocks which both gave our own fishermen priority and which made for effective conservation. This again would be extremely popular – at least in Britain.

Third, we would need to withdraw from all the entanglements into which we have been drawn by the pursuit of a common foreign and security policy and by common defence. It is likely that by the time of renegotiation substantial British forces will, if Mr Blair has his way, have been placed under a European command with its own planning staff, military doctrine and priorities. Although we would seek to achieve disengagement with the least disruption to any existing missions and commitments, Britain must return to the position in which her forces are under her own or NATO's control – not Europe's.

Fourth, we must seek to achieve as far as possible the basic, sensible objectives of the European Single Market, that is common recognition of standards, and open markets free of subsidies, distortions and non-tariff barriers – but without over-regulation, abuse of powers by the Commission and unwelcome intrusions by the European Court. I say 'as far as possible' because, for all the reasons I have given earlier, it is not at all clear that such an option is available. It may be necessary to negotiate a new relationship which retains most though not all of the benefits of the Single Market, but without the presently accompanying drawbacks.

This in turn leads on to the fifth and final objective of our renegotiation: Britain must regain control of its trade policy. At present the EU negotiates in these matters on our behalf through the Common Commercial Policy. But what suits the EU as a whole, with its bloated agricultural sector, does not suit us. Our interests lie primarily in global not European markets – markets to which at present we have no special access except through the ordinary WTO rules. These markets have also over the years been expanding faster than those of Europe and seem likely in the long run to continue doing so.

We live in a world in which physical distance has become much less significant as a constraint on commerce. This is reflected in the way in which our trade is so great with countries outside Europe. Britain's non-EU trade is the highest as a proportion of total trade of any EU member. Services, the fastest-growing area of our exports, is a particularly important component of this. In 1999, Britain was the world's largest outward investor. The most popular location for British foreign investment is the United States.[53] America is also by far the single most important source of Britain's inward investment – something which is often obscured by an excessive preoccupation with Japanese investment and so with the well-known advocacy by some Japanese businessmen of British membership of the euro.

Once free to do so, we could reorientate our trade policy in order to take advantage of these national and global trends.

The process of renegotiation on the basis of these five objectives should not be too protracted. It will be evident to our partners that our goals cannot be met by a few marginal adjustments or promises of future reviews.

But it should be made clear right at the start that in order to secure our objectives we would be prepared, if it became necessary, unilaterally to withdraw from EU membership. This might seem at first sight a provocative tactic: but it actually makes

OVERSEAS INVESTMENT
British direct investment overseas, year end 1999

	£ (billions)	%
Germany	10.9	2.6
France	12.9	3
Italy	3.0	0.7
Holland	69.0	16.3
Ireland	27.2	6.4
(EU)	(150.2)	(35.5)
Switzerland	5.7	1.3
United States	185.4	43.8
(Americas)	(207.2)	(48.9)
Japan	3.7	0.9
(Asia)	(25.3)	(6.0)
Australia	9.4	2.2
Africa	9.9	2.3

Source: Office of National Statistics, 13 December 2000. Figures are for book value of net assets. Total: £423.3 billion

good sense. We will never be taken seriously in renegotiation if our partners are allowed to believe that in the end we will settle for whatever we are offered.

But we must then, of course, be willing to have our bluff called. For reasons outlined above, any major changes in the operation of the EU to make it an organisation congenial to Britain are not very likely to be forthcoming. It is only realistic

OVERSEAS INVESTMENT

Foreign direct investment in Britain, year end 1999

	£ (billions)	%
Germany	38.4	15.3
France	19.1	8.4
Italy	1.1	0.5
Holland	37.3	15.7
Ireland	2.6	1.1
(EU)	(103.7)	(45.6)
Switzerland	8.0	3.5
United States	90.2	39.7
(Americas)	(100.8)	(44.3)
Japan	3.1	1.4
(Asia)	(4.9)	(2.2)
Australia	5.0	2.2
Africa	1.1	0.5

Source: Office of National Statistics, 13 December 2000. Figures are for book value of net assets. Total: £227.4 billion

to expect that the outcome may well amount to Britain's leaving the EU as it will have developed by the time of the negotiations, and establishing new links with European and non-European countries on a different basis. We should wish to make any such parting of the ways as amicable as possible – but friendship is a two-way street, and it may be that resolution in the face of a good deal of Continental temperament will be required. Yet reason will eventually prevail, as it so often does in life, by way of self-interest. Once our partners understand that we are serious, they too will talk seriously about how to establish a new and more stable relationship which suits their interests and ours.

There are a range of possibilities open to us. The first is simply to pursue a policy of unilateral free trade. This option is, in fact, a good deal more logical and attractive than it at first sounds. Experience and economic theory alike show that free trade is the best way for a country to exploit its natural advantages. Tiny Hong Kong is a case in point. Hong Kong grew rich as a duty-free port which, levying virtually no import tariffs, and from having an extremely modest standard of living forty years ago, rose to enjoy a GDP per capita higher than that of the UK. Those willing to put their skills and resources to good use on the open international market have nothing to fear but fear itself.

It may be objected that a policy of unilateral free trade by Britain is politically unrealistic. And that may turn out to be right. Producers' interests can never be totally overcome by the interests of consumers. But the option is certainly worth discussing, not least because it exposes the fallacy that outside the EU Britain would be 'alone', 'isolated', 'excluded' and so on. Countries trade with each other – or to be more precise people buy and sell from each other across frontiers – because that is the way to advance their interests. We do not need to beg people to trade with us – as long as we have something that people want, of a quality they expect and at a price they are prepared to pay.

The second option is to seek to join NAFTA. I have advocated this course of action for some years, not just for economic but also strategic reasons – that is, as a way of strengthening the trans-Atlantic links of NATO. Originally, I envisaged the formation of a NAFTA (rechristened a North *Atlantic* Free Trade Area) in which an enlarged EU would participate, along with the United States, Canada and Mexico (the present NAFTA members). This is, in theory, still a possibility. But I am no longer convinced that it is a serious option. The EU shows no real interest in making the reforms which would be required to qualify. Moreover, Europe's centralising political ambitions have risen to the top of its agenda and seem likely for the fore-seeable future to remain there. As a result, the EU and NAFTA look less and less similar as the years go by.

It would, therefore, probably be preferable for Britain to join NAFTA under a separate agreement, something in which there is also serious interest in some quarters within the United States. For example, Senator Phil Gramm, until recently Chairman of the Senate Committee on Banking, Housing and Urban Affairs, has been at the forefront of calls for Britain to be included in NAFTA.[54]

NAFTA's advantages over the EU are numerous and significant. It has more and, on average, richer consumers than euro-land. Its economies have been growing faster. Its markets are more open and it has stronger links with the global economy. It is much less reliant on subsidies. It is more attractive to outside investors. Finally, it is also much better at creating jobs: since 1992 the number of jobs has risen by 38 per cent in Mexico, 13 per cent in Canada and the US, compared with just 3 per cent in euro-land.[55]

Perhaps most significant, however, is not just the potential of NAFTA as opposed to that of the EU: it is, rather, the fact that NAFTA is neither a customs union nor a political/admin-istrative entity with grand ambitions. It is simply what it says it is – an association dedicated to free trade. Membership of

NAFTA does not therefore inhibit a country from entering into trade relationships with other countries as and when it sees fit. And this leads to the third possibility – a global Free Trade Area (FTA).

This idea has been advanced by John Hulsman, a scholar at the Heritage Foundation, as constituting a 'new trading agenda for the age of globalisation'.[56] Dr Hulsman advocates Britain's entry into the FTA of which we and the United States would be charter members – along with Singapore, Bahrain, the Czech Republic and Chile among others. The framework of the organisation would be one within which the freest economies of the world – judged according to the criteria of freedom to trade, freedom to invest, freedom to operate a business, security of property rights – would come together voluntarily. Not only would this arrangement work to stimulate the members' prosperity: it would also act as a beacon and an example to others. And, like NAFTA, it would, of course, leave the member states free to manage their own affairs.

Either NAFTA or the global FTA or indeed any other free-trade organisation would allow Britain the liberty to negotiate a new trade relationship with the countries of the European Union. Ideally, of course, this would take place before Britain formally withdrew as a full member of the EU: no one wants more disruption than necessary. But whatever the circumstances, it would be right to try to keep some aspects of our present trading relationship. For the reasons given earlier, there is no doubt that the EU members would want such links. How *much* they wanted them would, within the overall WTO framework, decide how favourable to us the final arrangement would be.

There are, though, useful precedents. In 1992, Norway, Iceland and Liechtenstein – that is the remaining EFTA countries, bar Switzerland – concluded negotiations with the EU which established a European Economic Area (EEA). These countries now enjoy free trade with the European Union, that is the freedoms of movement of goods, of services, of people and of capital. They also enjoy the unhindered access guaranteed by the operation of the European Single Market. But they remain outside the customs union, the CAP, the CFP, the common foreign and security policy and the rest of the legal/bureaucratic tangle of EU institutions.

The main problem for these countries is that they are effectively required to implement all the EU Single Market directives without having a vote on the form those directives take. There is also a mechanism by which they are very strongly encouraged, if not actually forced, to accept European Court decisions on the interpretation of these rules. This is not a very satisfactory situation because the relationship is skewed in favour of the EU.

But Britain is in a different league from countries like Norway (population 4.4 million) or Iceland (population 270,000), let alone Liechtenstein (population thirty-two thousand). Their negotiating position hardly compares with that which Britain would enjoy with a population of 59.5 million and the second largest GDP in Europe. We could press for Britain to be represented in the drawing up of all Single Market legislation, even though we were not party to other EU functions – like the CAP – where of course we could not be represented.

The existing EEA is not now the only model available to us. A more comparable, and very recent, precedent is that set by Mexico, which is also, of course, a member of NAFTA. In November 1999 Mexico and the EU negotiated a free-trade agreement which is the most comprehensive ever entered into by the Europeans. It covers the free movement of goods (including agriculture) and services, intellectual property rights, investment, public procurement and competition. Like NAFTA, and unlike the EEA, it excludes, however, free movement of people.[57] The provisions relating to Single Market directives and their interpretation are more satisfactory. Mexico is not subject to the rulings of the European Court of Justice.

TRADE BLOCS
Trading associations: EU, EEA, EFTA, NAFTA, 2002

EU	EEA	EFTA	NAFTA
Austria	Austria	Iceland	Canada
Belgium	Belgium	Liechtenstein	Mexico
Britain	Britain	Norway	USA
Denmark	Denmark	Switzerland	
Finland	Finland		
France	France		
Germany	Germany		
Greece	Greece		
Holland	Holland		
Ireland	Ireland		
Italy	Italy		
Luxembourg	Luxembourg		
Portugal	Portugal		
Spain	Spain		
Sweden	Sweden		
	Iceland		
	Liechtenstein		
	Norway		

Trade disputes between the EU and Mexico will be negotiated by officials from each side, and if further resolution is required the matter goes for bilateral arbitration through the WTO.

Mexico is a large country (population ninety-five million) with a still larger potential for growth. But its economy is less than a third the size of Britain's. Whatever Mexico can achieve in obtaining a fair deal with the EU struck from outside, Britain can more than achieve from within – given our ability to cause trouble if we are not properly treated.

The Mexican example also provides a further model according to which a member of a dedicated free-trade area (NAFTA) can also enjoy free trade with a customs union (the EU). The theoretical problem of how to ensure that imports from third countries do not pass into the economy of one member of a free-trade area to be re-exported into another – which would undermine a country's ability to govern its trade relations with third countries – is solved. Thus, as with the EEA, agreed procedures will be established to determine 'rules of origin'. Typically, for a product which contains material that originates from outside the EU or Mexico, it must have undergone a significant amount of processing within the free-trade zone if it is to qualify for reduced or zero tariffs.

Such a system, it is true, has some drawbacks for trade; but they can easily be exaggerated. Although the rules relating to Mexico are more stringent on paper than those for the EEA, there is not much difference in practice. Provisions for 'approved exporters' smooth the movement of trade, and over recent years there have been large reductions for technical reasons in worldwide trade bureaucracy in any case.

Anyone who doubts that making a large free-trade area work is a practical proposition need only examine the successes of NAFTA. And, of course, such an approach has one enormous advantage – under it Britain would retain control over her own affairs and could, therefore, adapt her policies to her interests as events unfold.[58]

Finally, one should mention Switzerland, the only remaining member of EFTA not within the EEA. Switzerland is unique in many ways. But whatever Switzerland has secured in its dealings with Europe Britain too could certainly obtain without great difficulty. Switzerland enjoys free trade with the EU and has reached some 150 bilateral agreements. One of those awaiting ratification by the EU includes free movement of labour. The EFTA model is perhaps not ideal: but it is certainly an acceptable option. Moreover, when discussing the case of the Swiss and the EEA members we must remember that trade with Europe is far more important for them than for us. Britain is a truly global player.

All these matters are basically economic, and no worse for that: those who talk in a superior fashion of 'bread and butter issues' generally eat something better than bread and butter. Yet at the heart of our relationship with the other members of the EU and the EU institutions is a constitutional fact. However Britain's renegotiated relations with the EU turn out, the British Parliament will have to take back powers which have been lost through the Treaty of Rome, through subsequent treaty changes, and through the operation of the European Court of Justice and indeed the British courts. Without this exertion of parliamentary sovereignty, it would be impossible to recreate our relationship with Europe on a satisfactory basis.

It is sometimes suggested that Britain has no right to withdraw from the EU, if that is the route which – after a referendum – were to be chosen. And doubtless this is something which would be argued, at least in Europe. It is certainly true that neither the Treaty of Rome nor the Maastricht and other treaties contains any explicit secession or denunciation clauses. It is also true that, given the EU's determined acquisition of more and more powers pertaining to statehood, at some stage in the future development of the European Union into a super-state Britain might cease to be regarded in international law as a sovereign state in its own right. This view might even, given current trends in judicial thinking, at this final stage be echoed in British courts.

But we are not at that stage yet. The fundamental point to bear in mind now is that the UK is (in the language used by international lawyers) a 'dualist' rather than a 'monist' state. What this means is that international law is regarded in our domestic law as a separate legal system. International treaties thus do not (except in exceptional cases, and this is not one of them) give rise to legal rights or obligations which can be enforced in British courts of law. It follows from this that Britain does indeed possess the effective legal power to leave the EU – or to change the terms of its relationship with the EU – because Parliament can when it wishes terminate the enforceability of Community law in British courts.[59]

There is, though, a further point which should not be forgotten. No one has a higher view of law than I do. But laws have to be rooted in the hearts and minds of the people if they are to be authoritative. Ultimately, what determines where sovereignty lies is whether the authority of a state's constitutional government is sufficient to command the loyalty of its citizens or (in the British system) the obedience of its subjects.

That is not, of course, a hard and fast distinction – which is one reason why it is always a risky business to try to alter long-standing political institutions and shake the habits and attitudes built around them. But it can still be said without any shadow of doubt that the people of Britain believe that they live under the sovereign authority of their own constitutionally elected government rather than that of the EU. As long as this remains the case, the traditional doctrine of the sovereignty of Parliament (or more precisely of the monarch in Parliament) will hold good. Parliament's ultimate ability to make or unmake laws thus also remains.

It sometimes happens that almost overnight a course of action which has previously been dismissed as unthinkable becomes a matter of sheer commonsense. I witnessed just such a turnaround when as British Prime Minister after our 1979 election victory I led a government which up-ended Keynesian economic orthodoxy and substituted monetarist policies deemed unthinkable by the post-war political consensus. Ronald Reagan as US President experienced much the same. As he wryly put it, reflecting on America's economic renaissance: 'The best sign that our economic programme is working is that they didn't call it Reaganomics any more.'

I predict that it will eventually be the same with Europe. That such an unnecessary and irrational project as building a European superstate was ever embarked upon will seem in future years to be perhaps the greatest folly of the modern era. And that Britain, with her traditional strengths and global destiny, should ever have been part of it will appear a political error of historic magnitude. There is, though, still time to choose a different and a better course.

I believe, therefore, that:

- We in Britain should fundamentally reassess our relationship with the rest of the EU and renegotiate it in order to secure our national interests and sovereignty

- We should not rule out any particular framework, as long as it meets our stated objectives
- NAFTA seems likely to be the best trading association to join initially, given Britain's historic and continuing trans-Atlantic links, but other complementary free-trade arrangements may also emerge
- We trade globally, and we must think globally – not confined within the bounds of a narrow Europe.

Notes

Chapter 1: Europe – Dreams and Nightmares

1. Tony Blair, 'I'm a British Patriot', article in the *Sun*, 17 March 1997.
2. There are, it is true, debates about what 'federalism' means. The term has been used in America to mean restoring powers to the states which despite the provisions of the US Constitution have passed to the federal government. In Europe, federalism is usually understood in the light of the federalism of the Federal Republic of Germany, i.e. a state in which sovereignty is exercised by the central government with a degree of local autonomy. This is the sense in which I shall be using the term.
3. I am indebted to Jeffrey Gedmin for drawing my attention to this quotation.
4. Jean Monnet (1888–1979), French financier and high official, often regarded as the founding father of the European Common Market; Robert Schuman (1886–1963) – as French Foreign Minister he proposed the Schuman Plan which led to the European Coal and Steel Community; Alcide de Gasperi (1881–1954), Italian Prime Minister 1945–53; Paul Henri Spaak (1899–1972), alternately Belgian Prime Minister, Foreign Minister and international high official; Konrad Adenauer (1876–1967), first Chancellor of West Germany (1949–63).
5. Quoted by Luca Einaudi, *National Institute Economic Review*, April 2000.
6. Quoted in John Laughland's profound and revealing study of the origins of Euro-federalist thinking, *The Tainted Source: The Undemocratic Origins of the European Idea* (London, 1997), p.19.
7. Quoted by *Financial Times*, 31 December 1993.
8. Ludwig Erhard (1897–1977), West German Economics Minister 1949–63, Chancellor of West Germany 1963–66.

9. Oskar Lafontaine and Dominique Strauss-Kahn, *Le Monde*, 15 January 1999.

10. Keith Marsden, *Handicap, Not Trump Card: The Franco–German Model isn't Working* (Centre for Policy Studies, July 1999).

11. Bill Jamieson and Patrick Minford, *Britain and Europe: Choices for Change* (Politeia and Global Britain, 1999).

12. F.A. Hayek, *The Road to Serfdom* (London: Routledge and Kegan Paul, 1979), p.95.

13. Speech to the Friends of Europe, 6 February 2001.

14. Demographers regard the 'replacement rate', i.e. the fertility rate needed to see that the population stays the same, as being 2.1. In Italy Silvio Berlusconi's right-of-centre administration was trying to get to grips with the pensions crisis when it fell in 1994. He and his colleagues will now have the chance to try again: see p.33. These figures are drawn from Peter G. Peterson, *Gray Dawn: How the Coming Age Wave will Transform America and the World* (New York: Random House, 1999), pp.77–8.

15. Peterson, *Gray Dawn*, p.164. Actually, the first truly radical steps towards a national system of funded private pensions were made in Chile in 1981 – under the Pinochet government.

16. Niall Ferguson and Laurence J. Kotlikoff, 'The Degeneration of EMU', *Foreign Affairs*, March–April 2000.

17. The objectives of the CAP were outlined in the 1957 Treaty of Rome. It was designed 'to increase agricultural productivity', 'to ensure a fair standard of living for the agricultural community', 'to stabilise markets', 'to ensure the availability of supplies' and 'to ensure that supplies reach consumers at reasonable prices'. The CAP operates a free internal agricultural market without tariffs or quotas, but with a common system of external protection giving preference to European Community farmers. Farm-product prices are determined by the Council of Ministers, and maintained through export subsidies and intervention. For a full description of the workings of the CAP see Richard Howarth, 'The CAP: History and Attempts at Reform', in Linda Whetstone (ed.), *Reforming the CAP*, Institute of Economic Affairs, June 2000, pp.4–5.

18. Howarth, 'The CAP: History and Attempts at Reform', p.5.

19. Quoted by Graeme Leach, *EU Membership – What's the Bottom Line?*, Institute of Directors Policy Paper, March 2000.

20. The estimate is made by economists Brent Borrell and Lionel Hubbard and is quoted by Denise H. Froning and Aaron Schavey in 'How the United States and the European Union can Improve Cooperation on Trade', *Heritage Foundation Executive Memorandum*, 7 March 2001.

21. Quoted in 'Europe's Burden', *The Economist*, 22 May 1999.
22. The 'next wave' candidate countries are Bulgaria, the Czech Republic, Cyprus, Estonia, Hungary, Latvia, Lithuania, Malta, Romania, Poland, Slovakia, Slovenia.
23. 'Germany Goes Cool on Polish Hopes to Join EU', *The Times*, 10 October 2000.
24. English, French, German, Italian, Spanish (Castilian), Portuguese, Greek, Dutch, Swedish, Danish, Irish (Gaelic) and Finnish.
25. For example, a poll of European twenty-one-to-thirty-five-year-olds showed that only one out of three considers himself as European rather than as a national of his own country. There are, though, differences between nations: 40 per cent of young Italians thought of themselves as European first, but only 25 per cent of young British people. *Time Magazine* survey, 26 March 2001.
26. Besides their mother tongue, 41 per cent of Europeans claim to know English, compared with just 19 per cent French and 10 per cent German. Moreover, some 70 per cent of Europeans consider that everyone in the EU should be able to speak English. *Europeans and Languages*, Eurobarometer Report, 54, 15 February 2001.
27. Speech at the Humboldt University, Berlin, 12 May 2000. Interestingly, very similar sentiments have been expressed by that other former left-wing revolutionary, and now Green Party MEP, Daniel Cohn-Bendit; *Guardian*, 10 November 2000.
28. Speech to the German Bundestag, Berlin, 27 June 2000.
29. Chancellor Schröder's proposals are outlined in 'Responsibility for Europe', a draft document published by the Social Democratic Party of Germany, 30 April 2001.
30. Speech in Paris, 28 May 2001.
31. Speech by Tony Blair to the Polish Stock Exchange, Warsaw, 6 October 2000.
32. Findings from polls conducted by the Wickert Institute and *Stern* magazine, reported in *The Times*, 23 September 1992.
33. *Daily Telegraph*, 3 April 2001.
34. *The Times*, 27 April 1993.
35. *Daily Telegraph*, 16 March 2000.
36. The most recent spat between the Eurocracy and democracy is in Ireland, where after a majority voted in a referendum to reject the Nice Treaty the European Commissioner responsible for enlargement, Günter Verheugen, commented: 'Such a referendum in one country cannot block the biggest and most important project for the political and economic future of the united Europe' (*The Times*, 9 June 2001).

37. The three were: Martti Ahtisaari, the former Finnish President; Jochen Frowein, Director of the Max Planck Institute in Heidelberg; and Marcelino Oreja, the former Spanish Foreign Minister.
38. *The Times*, 19 February 2000.
39. Actually, the EU did not quite dare to do this in the case of Austria – knowing that no such breach existed – and so used the device of 'bilateral' sanctions by all individual EU countries to achieve the same end. A typical European fiddle.
40. The European Commission has opportunistically sought to gain rapid acceptance of these proposals on the back of the events of 11 September. But, as Martin Howe observes, '... current proposals for an EU-wide arrest warrant will do little to assist in the fight against terrorism and will serve to undermine the already inadequate substantive safeguards under the European Extradition Convention'. *Tackling Terrorism*, p.20.
41. Articles 29 and 31 of the Treaty on European Union, as amended and renumbered by the Treaty of Amsterdam.
42. Proposal for a Council Regulation establishing a general framework for Community activities to facilitate the implementation of a European judicial area in civil matters, presented by the Commission on 5 June 2001.
43. In the SPD document 'Responsibility for Europe' (30 April 2000), Chancellor Schröder suggested that Europol be developed into 'an operative European police force, equipped with executive authority'. In the speech he made in Paris on 28 May 2001, M. Jospin endorsed a similar approach.
44. For a discussion of the specific implications of the euro for Britain, see Chapter Two. The timetable for introduction of the euro by the twelve participating states – Belgium, Germany, Greece, Spain, France, Ireland, Italy, Luxembourg, The Netherlands, Austria, Portugal, Finland – is as follows: the European Central Bank (ECB) was set up by the end of 1998; conversion rates between the euro and the old national currencies (which alone circulated) were fixed on 1 January 1999, with the ECB setting a single interest rate; between 1 January 2002 and 30 June 2002 there will be dual circulation of both euros and national currencies; by 30 June 2002 national currencies are to have been withdrawn from circulation.
45. Quoted in *The Times*, 6 November 1997.
46. Speech at the Bundesbank, Frankfurt, 30 August 1999, quoted in the *Financial Times*, 31 August 1999.
47. Speech to the European Parliament, 12 January 1999, quoted in the *Daily Telegraph*, 13 January 1999.

48. Interview in *The Times*, 1 January 1999.
49. Article in *Frankfurter Allgemeine Zeitung*, 27 May 1998.
50. Speech in Paris, 28 May 2001.
51. Article 104b.
52. Joint Declaration issued at the British–French Summit, Saint-Malo, France, 3–4 December 1998.
53. At the press conference given by President George W. Bush and Prime Minister Tony Blair at Camp David on 23 February 2001, President Bush said: '[Mr Blair] assured me that the European defence would in no way undermine NATO. He also assured me that there would be a joint command, that the planning would take place within NATO, and that should all NATO not wish to go on a mission, that would then serve as a catalyst for the defence forces moving on their own.'
54. *Daily Telegraph*, 28 March 2001.
55. *Daily Telegraph*, 28 March 2001.
56. *Sunday Times*, 4 March 2001; *Daily Telegraph*, 12 April 2001.
57. Helmut Kohl in particular has been at the forefront of calls for a United States of Europe. For example: 'By the end of this century, the foundation stone will have been laid for a United States of Europe' (speech at Harvard University, reported in the *Boston Globe*, 8 June 1990).

Chapter 2: Britain and Europe – Time to Renegotiate

1. For example, former British Foreign Secretary Sir Geoffrey (now Lord) Howe in a speech to the Bow Group at the Conservative Party Conference in 1990: 'The next European train is about to leave, for a still undefined destination, but certainly in the direction of some form of EMU. Shall Britain be in the driver's cab this time or in the rear carriage?' (*The Times*, 12 October 1990). Also, Chancellor Helmut Kohl, addressing a meeting of the German Cabinet in 1992 following Denmark's rejection of the Maastricht Treaty: 'Everything must be done so that the European train is not halted' (*Daily Telegraph*, 5 June 1992).
2. What follows is based upon William Kenway's pamphlet 'European Union – The Moment of Truth', amended reprint from *European Journal*, 5/8–9, 1998, and upon the account of Britain's first application to join the Common Market in 1961 contained in the official papers now reproduced in Lionel Bell, *The Throw that Failed: Britain's Original Application to Join the Common Market* (London: New European Publications Ltd, 1995), pp.140–96.
3. Speech to the States-General of The Netherlands, The Hague, 9 May 1946.

4. Speech in the Albert Hall, London, 14 May 1947.
5. Quoted in Timothy Bainbridge (ed.), *The Penguin Companion to European Union* (London: Penguin, 2000), p.43.
6. Speech opening a debate on Foreign Affairs in the House of Commons, Hansard, 11 May 1953, Col. 891.
7. Andrew Roberts, 'Lies, Damn Lies', *Sunday Times*, 28 July 1996. I am also grateful to Mr Roberts for helping me locate these various Churchill texts.
8. See the account in *The Path to Power*, pp.87–91.
9. Quoted by Bell, *The Throw that Failed*, Appendix D, p.179.
10. Charles de Gaulle, speaking at a press conference, 14 January 1963. Quoted by Charles G. Cogan, *Charles de Gaulle: A Brief Biography with Documents* (Boston: St Martin's Press, 1996), pp.200–1.
11. Reginald Maudling (1917–79), President of the Board of Trade 1959–61, Colonial Secretary 1961–62, Chancellor of the Exchequer 1962–64, Home Secretary 1970–72. The Maudling Committee, appointed by the Organisation for European Economic Cooperation (OEEC) in 1959, laid the foundations for the establishment of the European Free Trade Association (EFTA) in 1960.
12. Enoch Powell (1912–98), Conservative MP 1950–74, Ulster Unionist MP 1974–87, Minister of Health 1960–63, Shadow Minister of Defence 1965–68.
13. Sir Con O'Neill, *Britain's Entry into the European Community: Report on the Negotiations of 1970–1972* (London: Frank Cass, 2000), p.355.
14. Edward Heath, speech to the House of Commons, Hansard, 25 February 1970, Col. 1221.
15. White Paper on *The United Kingdom and the European Communities*, HMSO Cmnd. 4715, July 1971, pp.8–9. Interestingly, Sir Edward Heath in a valedictory personal statement to the House of Commons has by implication placed a rather different interpretation on the contents of his White Paper twenty years later: 'My proudest achievement was to have successfully negotiated entry of the United Kingdom into the European Community … *In the modern world it is only right that we should share our sovereignty with our European neighbours … I have no doubt that a united Europe is here to stay*' (emphasis added). Hansard, 9 May 2001, Col. 116.
16. *Britain's New Deal in Europe*, official government leaflet circulated nationally at the time of the 1975 referendum campaign on membership of the European Community.
17. See *The Downing Street Years*, pp.60–4, 536–59, 727–67.

18. Office of National Statistics and 'European Finances: Statement on the 2000 EC Budget and measures to counter fraud and financial mismanagement', Cmnd. 4771. Figures at constant 1998 prices.

19. Paolo Cecchini (ed.), *1992, The European Challenge: The Benefits of a Single Market* (European Commission, 1988).

20. For a fuller account of these and connected events in Europe, see *The Downing Street Years*, pp.546–59.

21. For a balanced analysis see Leach, *EU Membership – What's the Bottom Line?*, pp.31–6.

22. Christopher Booker and Richard North, *The Castle of Lies: Why Britain Must Get Out of Europe* (London: Duckworth, 1996).

23. *Economist World in Figures, 2001.*

24. Jacques Delors (b.1925), French Finance Minister 1981–84, President of the European Commission 1985–94.

25. Under the Nice Treaty, British voting power in the European Council of Ministers will be reduced from 11.5 per cent to 8.4 per cent with enlargement to a twenty-seven-member European Union.

26. The Luxembourg Compromise was introduced by the Six in January 1966, and remained in use until the mid-1980s, though it was never officially recognised by the European Commission and the European Court of Justice. I called for its reintroduction in a speech in the House of Lords in July 1992.

27. I am delighted that the new leader of the Conservative Party, Iain Duncan Smith – a patriot to his fingertips – seems to agree.

28. Luckily, one such genius, Noel Malcolm, has demolished the wrong arguments and advanced the right one in his pamphlet *Sense on Sovereignty* (Centre for Policy Studies, 1991).

29. This was an allusion to the fact that the Prime Minister and his colleagues had been warning of a return to the Tory years of 'boom and bust'. Actually, there was a great deal more boom than bust, but that is another story.

30. 'Tony Blair is Committed to the Extinction of Britain', *Daily Telegraph*, 1 June 2001.

31. Interview with Daniel Hannan, 'Yes, You can Leave', *Spectator*, 27 May 2000.

32. *The Times*, 26 April 1997.

33. See *The Downing Street Years*, p.724.

34. UNCTAD World Investment Report 2000. Sweden, also outside the euro-zone, was the second-largest recipient of non-EU foreign investment.

35. *What Would the Euro Cost UK Business?*, House of Commons Trade and Industry Select Committee Report, 7 November 2000.

The figures are based on studies carried out by KPMG Consulting and Chantrey Vellacott DFK.

36. A May 2001 MORI poll for the *Sun* for example showed 70 per cent of respondents opposed to a European single currency and just 24 per cent in favour. In an ICM poll for the *Guardian* conducted in the same month, 67 per cent of those interviewed declared they would vote 'no' in a referendum on the euro.

37. This view was exemplified by remarks by the then Foreign Secretary Robin Cook, who on being reminded of the hostility to the euro shown in opinion polls replied: 'I welcome the fact that in those opinion polls which show the majority of the public are against joining the euro, they all show the same two-thirds majority believe joining the euro is inevitable.' *The Times*, 7 July 2000.

38. A BBC *Today* poll conducted by ICM in January 2001 showed 53 per cent of respondents thinking that Britain should stay in the EU, 30 per cent wanting to leave, and 16 per cent 'didn't know'. A *Sun* poll conducted by MORI in April/May 2001 asked: 'If there were a referendum now on whether Britain should stay in or get out of the EU, how would you vote?' Forty-eight per cent wanted to stay in, 43 per cent wanted to get out, and 9 per cent 'didn't know'.

39. Office of National Statistics and 'European Finances: Statement on the 2000 EC Budget and measures to counter fraud and financial mismanagement', Cmnd. 4771. Figures at constant 1998 prices.

40. Norman Lamont, *Sovereign Britain* (Bristol: Duckworth, 1995), p.86.

41. Patrick Minford, *Britain and Europe: The Balance Sheet*, Centre for European Studies and European Business Review, MCB University Press, 1996, p.3. Professor Minford has kindly provided me with an updated figure. A study by Ruth Lea of the Institute of Directors gave a similar figure of £9–£10 billion for the cost of the CAP to the British economy. She points out that in 1999, British taxpayers subsidised other farmers in the EU by about £2 billion (Ruth Lea, *CAP: A Catalogue of Failure. The Need for Radical Reform*, IOD Research Paper, November 2000, p.6).

42. This and other connected matters were discussed in illuminating fashion by Martin Wolf, 'Thinking the Unthinkable', *Financial Times*, 18 June 1996. Imperial Preference was a system of preferential tariff rates operated between Britain and her colonies between 1932 and the end of Empire in the 1960s.

43. Nigel Pain and Garry Young, *Continent Cut Off ? The Macroeconomic Impact of British Withdrawal from the EU*, National Institute of Economic and Social Research, February 2000.

44. Keith Vaz, interview with the *Daily Telegraph*, 19 February 2000.
45. I am grateful to Dr Brian Hindley for allowing me sight of the draft introduction of the revision of the booklet written by him and Martin Howe, *Better Off Out?: The Benefits or Costs of EU Membership* (IEA, 1996). Dr Hindley points out that the adverse effects on inward investment are much exaggerated and notes that the US International Trade Commission report in 2000 describes them as 'small'.
46. Minford, *Britain and Europe: The Balance Sheet*, p.33.
47. Speech to the 'Global Panel', The Hague, 15 May 1992. *Collected Speeches*, no. 51.
48. *The Path to Power*, p.502.
49. *The Path to Power*, pp.504–5.
50. *UK Trade Statistics 1998*, Office of National Statistics.
51. I am not, though, going to pretend that official free-trade agreements with Europe will ever lead in practice to full free-trade access. Europe's non-tariff barriers, such as anti-dumping duties or their threat, which protect, for example, computers and other durables, would work against us. But then perfectly free trade, like other perfect things, is rarely attainable in practice. I am grateful to Patrick Minford for reminding me of this qualification.
52. In the 'Factortame' case, ninety-seven Spanish fishermen were awarded £55 million compensation in February 2001 after the European Court ruled that the British government had unfairly discriminated against foreign trawlermen through the 1988 Merchant Shipping Act. The case was brought against Britain by a consortium of Spanish fishing-vessel owners, led by the Spanish-owned company Factortame Ltd, who claimed they had been unable to register their ships to operate in British waters.
53. Jamieson and Minford, *Britain and Europe*, pp.73–4.
54. 'Euroland and NAFTA: The View from Across the Atlantic', speech by Senator Phil Gramm to the Centre for Policy Studies, 4 July 2000.
55. Keith Marsden, *Towards 'A Treaty of Commerce': Euroland and Nafta Compared* (Centre for Policy Studies, July 2000), p.19.
56. John C. Hulsman, *The World Turned Rightside Up: A New Trading Agenda for the Age of Globalisation*, with commentaries by Patrick Minford, Martin Howe, David Davis and Bill Jamieson, Institute of Economic Affairs, 2001.
57. This 'freedom' has in any case always been problematic in view of the need to apprehend terrorists and other criminals and to curb illegal immigration and bogus asylum seeking. In this matter, NAFTA perhaps offers a better model than the EEA.

58. The details and the implications of this agreement are analysed by Ronald Stewart-Brown in 'The Mexico–EU Free Trade Agreement', *Global Britain Briefing Note*, 8, 2 June 2000. I am grateful to Mr Stewart-Brown for his very helpful explanation of the intricacies of the EU–Mexico FTA.
59. I am grateful to Martin Howe QC for his advice on these matters.